History of Vietnam

An Enthralling Overview from Ancient Times to Modern Days

© Copyright 2025 - All rights reserved.

The content contained within this book may not be reproduced, duplicated, or transmitted without direct written permission from the author or the publisher.

Under no circumstances will any blame or legal responsibility be held against the publisher, or author, for any damages, reparation, or monetary loss due to the information contained within this book, either directly or indirectly.

Legal Notice:

This book is copyright protected. It is only for personal use. You cannot amend, distribute, sell, use, quote, or paraphrase any part, or the content within this book, without the consent of the author or publisher.

Disclaimer Notice:

Please note the information contained within this document is for educational and entertainment purposes only. All effort has been executed to present accurate, up-to-date, reliable, and complete information. No warranties of any kind are declared or implied. Readers acknowledge that the author is not engaging in the rendering of legal, financial, medical, or professional advice. The content within this book has been derived from various sources. Please consult a licensed professional before attempting any techniques outlined in this book.

By reading this document, the reader agrees that under no circumstances is the author responsible for any losses, direct or indirect, that are incurred as a result of the use of the information contained within this document, including, but not limited to, errors, omissions, or inaccuracies.

Free limited time bonus

Stop for a moment. We have a free bonus set up for you. The problem is this: we forget 90% of everything that we read after 7 days. Crazy fact, right? Here's the solution: we've created a printable, 1-page pdf summary for this book that you're reading now. All you have to do to get your free pdf summary is to go to the following website: https://livetolearn.lpages.co/enthrallinghistory/

Or, Scan the QR code!

Once you do, it will be intuitive. Enjoy, and thank you!

Table of Contents

INTRODUCTION: THE STORY OF VIETNAM 1
CHAPTER 1: FROM PREHISTORIC TIMES TO THE DONG SON CULTURE 4
CHAPTER 2: THE VAN LANG AND AU LAC KINGDOMS 8
CHAPTER 3: CHINA AND THE QUEST FOR INDEPENDENCE 12
CHAPTER 4: THE LY AND TRAN DYNASTIES 17
CHAPTER 5: FRENCH CONQUEST OF VIETNAM 31
CHAPTER 6: THE COLONIAL RULE OF FRENCH INDOCHINA 45
CHAPTER 7: VIETNAM BETWEEN THE WORLD WARS 54
CHAPTER 8: THE JAPANESE OCCUPATION DURING WORLD WAR II 60
CHAPTER 9: THE AUGUST REVOLUTION AND THE FIRST INDOCHINA WAR 65
CHAPTER 10: THE VIETNAM WAR: A NATION DIVIDED 71
CHAPTER 11: REUNIFICATION AND THE PATH TO MODERNIZATION 85
CONCLUSION: WHAT DOES THE FUTURE HOLD FOR VIETNAM? 93
HERE'S ANOTHER BOOK BY ENTHRALLING HISTORY THAT YOU MIGHT LIKE 95
FREE LIMITED TIME BONUS 96
FURTHER READING AND REFERENCES 97
IMAGE SOURCES 98

Introduction:
The Story of Vietnam

In the very beginning of Vietnam's history, one will find a strong and vibrant nation that sought to chart its own course in the world. Through the years, though, Vietnam's ability to do so was often hampered and curtailed by outside powers. This has become a continuing trend throughout the history of this nation.

It seems that there were almost always others who thought they knew how to run Vietnam much better than the Vietnamese themselves. China, in particular, looms large in this role. For a large chunk of Vietnam's history, Vietnam existed as a vassal state of China.

The Chinese did not necessarily treat the Vietnamese badly (at least not all the time), but they most certainly did whatever they could to stunt any nationalistic sense of Vietnamese growth. After the legendary Lady Trieu led a revolt against the Chinese in 248 CE, the Chinese did what they could to stamp out the memory of her defiance.[1] The fact that she is remembered at all is in itself a demonstration of the fortitude of the Vietnamese.

Vietnam is a country that has largely been in the shadows and has largely been misunderstood. Even the name that is customarily used by Westerners is not quite right. The Vietnamese do not call their country "Vietnam" but rather the two-word variation of Việt Nam. This follows

---

[1] Ngoc, Huu. *Vietnam: Tradition and Change.* 2016. Pg. 95.

the same pattern as other Vietnamese place names such as Sài Gòn and Hà Nội.

The term "Việt" is in reference to the largest ethnic group in the nation, the Viet people, who make up a large majority of the population. The term "Nam" means "south." Put together, Việt Nam is basically a reference to the Viet people of the south.

During the Cold War, Vietnam was split between north and south, with American troops fighting alongside the South Vietnamese against the communist North Vietnamese. But the phrase "Viet of the South" predates that modern divide by many centuries. In older times, Việt Nam referred to the Viet people living south of China's core territories. Much earlier still, various Viet-related peoples inhabited lands now within southern China, in what are today the provinces of Guangxi and Guangdong. Over the centuries, Chinese expansion absorbed those northernmost areas, leaving the heartland of the Viet farther to the south—what we now recognize as Vietnam.

Nevertheless, the unique essence of the term has not been lost, just as the unique essence of what Vietnam means as a nation has not been lost, despite all of the many changes it has undergone throughout its history. Vietnam has witnessed independence and has been a vassal of China and a colony of France. It has been a nation split along ideological lines (split right at the 17th parallel) and is today a fully fledged communist state.

Yet, there is a thread of Vietnamese identity that can be found within all of those layers. At the core of Vietnamese society is the village. Vietnam has always been a network of villages, which in the French language (something Vietnam later adopted) are called "communes." Yes, it is indeed somewhat ironic that the French seemed to have prepped the Vietnamese in advance for a "communist" takeover since it was the French who introduced the term commune into the Vietnamese lexicon.[2] Communist ideologues took the term from the French in the first place and made use of it to describe a self-sufficient community that followed the precepts of communist founder Karl Marx. Marx himself borrowed heavily from radical socialist ideas conceived during the chaos of the French Revolution.

---

[2] Ngoc, Huu. *Vietnam: Tradition and Change.* Pg. 14.

The notion of communism itself being a network of interconnected villages was also clearly expressed in the early Soviet Union with its own communes, which were dubbed "soviets." These soviets were scattered all over Russian territory, and these communes came together under Russian dictators, such as Lenin, Stalin, Khruschev, Brezhnev, and the like.

In Vietnam, the French introduction of the term commune, the advent of communism, and its seemingly ready-made application to Vietnamese villages were just many things coming full circle. And that sense of coming right back to where one started is indeed the overarching story of Vietnam.

Chapter 1: From Prehistoric Times to the Dong Son Culture

"The brook rippling beneath the bridge is pure. The roadside grass is still a tender green. Seeing him off leaves her anguished. Once he's astride his horse, abroad his boat. The rushing water can never cleanse her grief. The fragrant grass can never ease her memories."

-*Vietnamese poet Chinh Phu Nham*[3]

    It is a simple truth to say that human history goes back much further than recorded history. Recorded history spans, at most, around five thousand years. If we go back further than that, we enter into the shadowy prehistoric past, of which there is only the faintest of legends and ancestral recollections, along with a scattering of artifacts, to try to piece together what happened.

    As is often the case with ancient lands whose origins stretch back into prehistory, the people of Vietnam have their own fanciful foundation story. According to Vietnamese legend, Vietnam came into being when a certain king named Lạc Long Quân, who was the Dragon Lord of the Mighty Seas, married a fair princess by the name of Âu Cơ, who just so happened to be the daughter of the Immortals of the High Mountains. They had one hundred children (some myths say they were all sons). Over time, the Dragon Lord and the Immortal Princess somehow became unhappy with each other and decided to go their separate ways.

---

[3] Ngoc, Huu. *Vietnam: Tradition and Change.* Pg. 8.

According to legend, half of their one hundred children followed the mother north over the mountains into what is now China, and the other half went with their father south past the mountains and toward the eastern sea to form Vietnam. It is furthermore suggested that the eldest child became king of Van Lang, a mythical Vietnamese kingdom.

Legends, of course, are not history but the half-forgotten musings of a people who came before anyone bothered to write anything down. The prehistory of Vietnam might stretch back as far as twenty thousand years. While we might be able to understand a few thousand years of Vietnamese history, the vast majority of what happened in this region remains in the shadows of prehistory.

At any rate, twenty thousand years ago, bands of hunter-gatherers arrived in the region. As was the case in many other parts of the world, they began to settle down, and at some point, they discovered agriculture. The fact that no single people group can claim to have invented agriculture is indicative of its utility and commonality. It seems that agriculture naturally emerged all over the planet wherever humans inhabited. It was likely a common-sense discovery made by our ancestors. Early humans observed how consumed fruits and veggies (excreted seeds encased in natural, human-made fertilizer) would sprout into plants that produced more fruits and veggies.

Such things might sound crude, but the simple fact that humans are even able to jump to such conclusions separates humans from animals. Beasts graze in the field, entirely oblivious as to how they might be able to plant and grow more grass.

As it pertains to Vietnam, we know that, just like today, the people of its prehistoric past cultivated rice. Vietnam's warm, wet Southeast Asian climate is perfect for wet-rice farming, and archaeological evidence suggests such cultivation was underway in the Red River Delta as far back as 2000 BCE.

Over time, this agricultural base helped give rise to the Dong Son culture, which flourished from around 1000 BCE to the first centuries of the Common Era. Centered in the fertile floodplains and lowlands of what is now northern Vietnam, the Dong Son are remembered for their abundant rice harvests, mastery of bronze casting, and striking ceremonial drums.

Dong Sun ceremonial drum.[1]

One unique thing about the early Vietnamese was their belief that a dragon from the skies supplied rain for their rice. When rain was scarce, these people would pull out large, magnificent bronze drums and beat on them in unison in order to get the sky dragon's attention. It is not clear how they developed this idea, but apparently, they beat on the bronze drums until it rained and their rice cultivation could begin anew. Bronze drums would come to symbolize ancient Vietnam, just as bronze incense burners have come to symbolize ancient China.[4]

The part of Vietnam inhabited by these early Vietnamese people was largely along the coast within the vicinity of two large delta regions. In the northern reaches near China, the Dong Son culture flourished. These leaders held authority over the land and the people, while rice farmers worked tirelessly in the fields. As rice farming expanded, the need for

---

[4] Ngoc, Huu. *Vietnam: Tradition and Change.* Pg. 30.

more laborers grew, contributing to the prosperity of these early agricultural societies.

Around this time, the legendary kingdom of Van Lang emerged under the rule of the Hung Kings. Later, in the 3rd century BCE, the kingdom of Au Lac was established when King An Duong Vuong unified the local tribes into a more centralized state.

Chapter 2: The Van Lang and Au Lac Kingdoms

"I want to ride the tempests, tame the waves, and behead the sharks in the East Sea. I want to exterminate the enemy, protect our borders, and save our people from the misery of slavery. I do not want a life of bowing my head and bending my back as a concubine."

-Lady Trieu[5]

In the northern reaches of what is now Vietnam, along the fertile banks of the Red River Delta, the Dong Son culture thrived. Known for its intricate bronze drums and advanced metalwork, this ancient society laid the groundwork for the region's first major kingdoms. The people of the Dong Son were skilled rice farmers, blacksmiths, and warriors. Their leaders oversaw large communities that grew in both size and sophistication. These early Vietnamese societies were not yet states in the modern sense, but they showed clear signs of organized leadership, agriculture-based economies, and increasingly complex social hierarchies.

According to legend, this region was once ruled by the fabled Hung Kings, who presided over a kingdom called Van Lang. The Hung dynasty is said to have lasted for nearly two millennia, beginning with Kinh Duong Vuong and continuing through a long line of successors. While much of this era is shrouded in myth, it reflects the Vietnamese people's deep reverence for their origins and their early sense of identity.

---

[5] Ngoc, Huu. *Vietnam: Tradition and Change*. Pg. 95.

Around the 3rd century BCE, however, a major shift occurred. A new group known as the Au Viet—mountain people from the northwest, likely tied to the Baiyue tribes of southern China—migrated southward into the Red River Delta. They came into contact with the local Lac Viet, the dominant ethnic group of Van Lang. While the precise details are murky, tradition holds that tensions rose between these two groups, culminating in a military campaign led by an ambitious Au Viet leader named Thuc Phan.

According to popular accounts, Thuc Phan's invasion might have been sparked by a rejected marriage alliance with the Van Lang royal family. Whether fact or folklore, it is said that he rallied a formidable army and marched south to confront the Hung Kings. The last of these kings, known in some records as Hung Vuong XVIII, was defeated, and Van Lang fell. Thuc Phan then unified the Au Viet and Lac Viet peoples under a new kingdom: Au Lac.

Now calling himself An Duong Vuong, Thuc Phan established a new capital at Co Loa, a remarkable spiral-shaped citadel located just north of present-day Hanoi. This massive structure, with its concentric walls and defensive design, was a symbol of centralized power and military innovation. Legends speak of sentries on the ramparts, archers guarding the gates, and even a magic crossbow gifted by the gods; the reality was likely impressive enough on its own, though. Co Loa served as a political center and a stronghold against outside threats.

King An Duong Vuong.²

However, Au Lac's independence would be short-lived. Just decades later, in 207 BCE, a former Qin general named Zhao Tuo (known in Vietnamese as Trieu Da) established his own kingdom to the north, called Nanyue (or Nam Viet). Initially based in modern-day Guangzhou, Trieu Da declared himself king and quickly expanded his reach into northern Vietnam. In 179 BCE, his forces invaded and annexed Au Lac, absorbing it into his growing realm.

Some scholars consider this conquest the beginning of Chinese domination in Vietnam, though the reality is more nuanced. The Trieu dynasty, while based in southern China, operated independently of the main Chinese empire and maintained a hybrid culture that blended local and Han Chinese elements. It wasn't until 111 BCE—when the Han dynasty fully annexed Nanyue—that imperial China established direct control over Vietnamese territory.

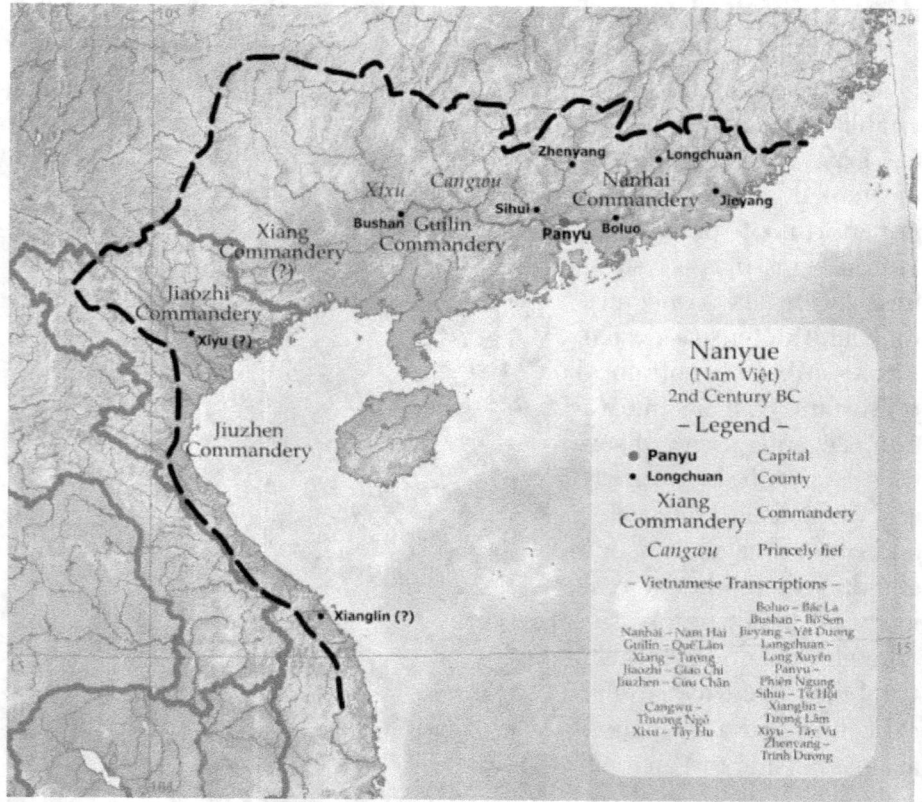

Nanyue.⁸

By that point, Han armies had advanced deep into the Red River Delta and beyond, reaching as far south as what is now Quang Binh Province. This marked the beginning of nearly a thousand years of Chinese influence and intermittent rule over the Vietnamese heartland—a legacy that would profoundly shape the region's political, cultural, and linguistic development.

Chapter 3: China and the Quest for Independence

"Henceforth our country is safe. Our mountains and rivers begin life afresh. Peace follows war as day follows night. Peace follows war as day follows night. We have purged our shame for a thousand centuries. We have regained tranquility for ten thousand generations."

-Ngu-yen Trai[6]

In the 2nd century BCE, China invaded Vietnam. The southernmost reaches of Vietnam remained independent, but all of northern Vietnam was taken over by the Chinese. China would lay claim to this land for well over one thousand years.

That is not to say there were not periodic uprisings against the Chinese. As much as uprisings, revolts, and guerrilla warfare have been ascribed to the Vietnamese in more recent history (mainly due to the Vietnam War), the Vietnamese actually have quite a long history of battling larger occupying powers. Before they engaged in guerrilla warfare in the 20th century, they engaged in it with China. All throughout the one-thousand-year Chinese occupation (talk about a long occupation!), Vietnamese freedom fighters periodically rose up in (often vain) attempts to throw off the Chinese yoke.

One of the most famous of these rebellions was led by the Trung sisters—Trung Trac and Trung Nhi—around the year 40 CE. These two

---

[6] Karnow, Stanley. *Vietnam: A History.* 1997. Pg. 116.

women came from the upper levels of Vietnamese society and were uniquely positioned to rally an armed uprising against Chinese rule.

While many others of their class focused on calligraphy and courtly refinement, the Trung sisters appear to have been trained in both the literary and martial arts. Whether this training came from their family or tutors is not certain, but what is clear is that they were skilled warriors and determined leaders.

Trung sisters.⁴

Although the achievements of the Trung sisters were remarkable, it should be noted that female leaders were not entirely unusual in Vietnam during this period. In many ways, Vietnam stood apart from its neighbors. Indigenous customs shaped by centuries of village life and clan-based organization gave women a more prominent role in public life than was common elsewhere in East and Southeast Asia. Women could inherit property, lead troops, and act as heads of communities. These rights and responsibilities were rarely afforded to their counterparts in surrounding cultures.

Trung Trac was married to a Vietnamese general by the name of Thi Sach. Thi Sach became incensed when the Chinese began demanding increased taxes on salt, as well as additional bribes, which were extorted by Vietnamese officials. Outraged, he began to openly speak of rebellion with his colleagues. He led a failed uprising, was captured, and subsequently killed by the Chinese. After his death, his wife, Trung Trac, along with her sister, Trung Nhi, rose up and cobbled together an even more massive revolt against the Chinese. This rebel army would eventually have as many as eighty thousand troops at its disposal.

The losses among the Vietnamese were quite heavy. The battlefields of northern Vietnam were covered in blood. As bloody as later conflicts in the region might have been, this particular conflict, even though it lacked the devastation of bombs, machine guns, and napalm, was just as terrible.

Interestingly, the Trung sisters were not the only women in their family leading the armies of Vietnam. Their mother was also a commander during this struggle, along with several other high-ranking women. They helped coordinate and, at times, even took part in the struggle to overthrow the Chinese yoke.

As much as they struggled against the Chinese occupation, there was no easy end in sight for the Vietnamese. At times, it likely seemed as if they were beating their heads against an insurmountable wall.

Nevertheless, the Vietnamese army—armed with bows and arrows, spears, swords, and battleaxes—rallied and overran a string of Chinese fortresses. At one point, they even forced the Han governor to withdraw from the region. In the wake of this triumph, Trung Trac was acclaimed as ruler of the Lac Viet lands, a position often described in later tradition as that of a queen. However, the victory was short-lived, and the respite from Han rule would not last.

After Chinese troops were driven out, it was only a matter of time before they would come back. It took just a few months for the Chinese to recalibrate, swell their forces in the south, and prepare themselves for a renewed invasion of Vietnam. In 41 CE, the emperor of China's Han dynasty, Guangwu, sent his forces into Vietnam to reclaim the region for China.

The battle was long and nasty. It dragged on until the Trung sisters were defeated in 43 CE. It is not clear what happened to the Trung sisters after their army was defeated. Some legends state that they threw themselves into a river, preferring to drown rather than be captured. However, other sources seem to indicate that they were captured and later executed by the Han.

Whatever happened to them, their legend would live on in the minds of many Vietnamese. They would become both martyrs and national symbols of future resistance.

However, as much as the Chinese were disliked for lording it over the Vietnamese during this time, Chinese contributions to Vietnamese culture were of tremendous importance. The introduction of Chinese farming implements, the domestication of livestock, and innovative rice irrigation techniques would prove crucial for the expansion of the Vietnamese civilization.

That is not to say that China deserves all of the credit for early Vietnamese rice cultivation—the Vietnamese began producing rice on their own. However, Chinese farming tools and irrigation techniques greatly improved the yield of Vietnamese rice paddy fields. Thanks to the Chinese, rice became a widespread and dependable resource. It remains a major staple of the Vietnamese diet to this day.

Now, fast forward some two hundred years, and another popular revolt transpired. This popular resistance movement took place around 248 CE and was led by a Vietnamese woman named Trieu Thi Trinh. Her brother, Trieu Quoc Dat, also joined her.

Trieu Thi Trinh would later be revered as simply the great "Lady Trieu." She is remembered for her tremendous effort to topple Chinese rule. After French colonization and the introduction of French history and literature, Lady Trieu was often conflated with the French heroine of old, Joan of Arc. Popular imagery of her depicts a fierce-eyed woman seated on top of a battle elephant with long hair streaming past her shoulders as she rallies the rebels to continue the fight against the Chinese. This revolt was ultimately crushed. The Wu dynasty sent in around eight thousand troops to put down the rebellion.

By the late 2nd century CE, as the Han dynasty weakened, a new power was quietly taking form. However, this power did not come from the north but rather along Vietnam's central coast. In 192 CE, a local leader named Khu Lien led a revolt in the former Han-controlled region of Rinan (Tuong Lam) and established a new kingdom. It was known to the Chinese as Lam Ap and later as Champa.

Positioned around what is now Da Nang and stretching along the central coastline, Champa stood apart from the Chinese-influenced north. Instead, it became deeply rooted in Indian maritime culture. It was a realm where Hindu and Buddhist ideas, Sanskrit inscriptions, and temple architecture flourished.

In fact, Champa was one of the first Southeast Asian polities to draw from both Indian and Southeast Asian traditions. Even though China maintained control over northern Vietnam for centuries, the central and southern regions under the Cham Kingdom remained independent and resilient. In 605 CE, the Sui dynasty launched a notable invasion against the Kingdom of Lam Ap (an early form of Champa), briefly subjugating the region before Cham forces regained their autonomy.

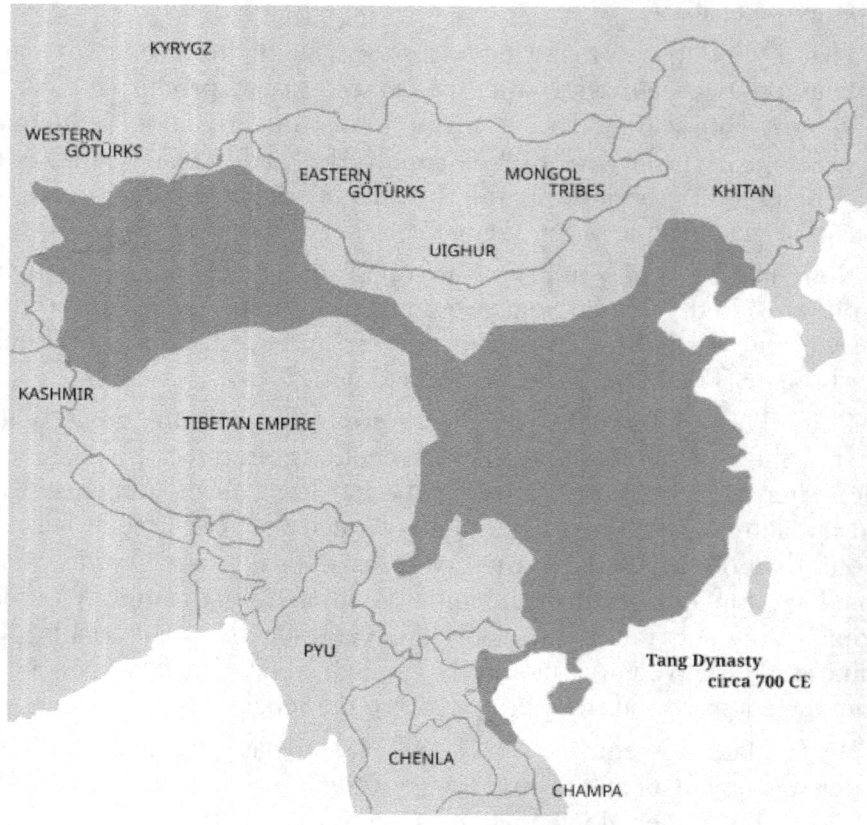

Vietnam under the Tang dynasty.[5]

Meanwhile, northern Vietnam remained under Chinese rule—first as part of the Tang-controlled Jiaozhi province and later through other Chinese dynasties. The situation changed dramatically in 939 CE when Ngo Quyen, a Vietnamese prefect, defeated the Chinese Southern Han fleet in a decisive battle at the Bach Dang River. He then declared independence, establishing himself as ruler and reinstating a new capital at Co Loa.

Chapter 4: The Ly and Tran Dynasties

"Ly Thuong Kiet knew how to overcome force by surprise, oppose his strong points against the enemy's weak points, pitch his well-rested troops against the enemy's weary soldiers, apply patience to arrogance, and particularly, how to rely on our people's determination to survive."

-*Vietnamese historian Hoang Xuan Han*[7]

Around the fateful year of 1009 CE, a Vietnamese ruler by the name of Le Long Dinh perished. In his place, a simple commander of the palace guard named Ly Cong Uan was selected by the royal court to take his place. This man, who would take the name Ly Thai To, would go on to found the Ly dynasty. Historians mark this as the beginning of one of Vietnam's great epochs—a period that would see the establishment of Thang Long as the capital, the flourishing of Buddhism, and the political foundations on which later dynasties would build. That such a transformative era began under a man of modest background speaks to the unique nature of the Ly dynasty.

Ly Thai To is credited with moving the capital from its old site of Hoa Lu to a new one in Dai La (modern-day Hanoi). He did this in 1010. Dai La was said to have later been renamed "Thang Long," which means "Ascending Dragon." This was due to the fact that Ly Thai To allegedly saw a dragon shoot up into the air from the area as soon as he

---

[7] Ngoc, Huu. *Vietnam: Tradition and Change*. Pg. 97.

arrived. Ly was a visionary, and it is said that at one time, he was privy to a vision that left an incredible mark on him and his subsequent successors. Ly is said to have dreamed that he somehow found himself face to face with the Vietnamese goddess of mercy, Quan The Am Bo Tat.

In the dream, the goddess was peacefully perched on a lotus flower when she suddenly presented to him a baby boy, which she had been holding in her hands. This meant a lot to Ly since he was getting older and had not yet produced an heir to the throne with whom he could entrust the continuity of his kingdom.

Ly was encouraged by the dream, and shortly after, he fell in love with a young lady who was a commoner. He married the girl, seemingly on the spur of the moment, and she eventually produced the male heir that Ly craved. For Ly, it seemed that the child the goddess of mercy had promised him in his dreams had materialized in the waking world.

According to tradition, Ly had the famed One Pillar Pagoda constructed in Hanoi as an expression of thanks. The wooden pagoda rests on a single stone pillar and is said to be built to mimic the dream imagery of Ly seeing the goddess perched upon a single lotus blossom. The roof of the pagoda, with its majestic upturned corners, is supposed to make one think of the petals of a flower.

The One Pillar Pagoda.⁶

The One Pillar Pagoda was meant to be a symbol of hope during times of difficulty, and the Vietnamese revered it as such. But interestingly enough, the French, who fought bitter wars with the Vietnamese, attempted to stave off the communist insurgents who wished to be free of their colonial overlords by purposefully targeting the One Pillar Pagoda. Just before the beaten and battered French abandoned Hanoi in 1954, they destroyed the pagoda.

As testament to the determination of the Vietnamese people, in whose hearts hope truly springs eternal, they rebuilt the structure very quickly. The wooden pagoda can still be seen perched upon that pillar to this very day.

Ly Thai To would rule until his passing in 1028. He then left it up to his successors to continue to build upon the principles that he had established, namely the idea that a ruler should be the caretaker for the people and to maintain a strong centralized state that could stand up to external threats. For instance, the capital had become a defensive bulwark, as it was focused primarily on enabling a sound and robust defense. This allowed his successors to move their focus away from military defense, allowing them to focus more on trade and fortifying the economy.

The third ruler of this dynasty, Ly Thanh Tong, renamed the nation Dai Viet. Ly Thanh Tong was a very interesting and innovative figure in Vietnamese history. He established the Temple of Literature, or as it would be called in Vietnamese, Van Mieu, in Hanoi in 1070. It was open to the public, and it was meant to be a center of learning. Serving as a kind of public library and a rudimentary university, the Temple of Literature became a hub of scholarly activity in Vietnam. Coursework at the temple would eventually evolve to include classes in literary composition, which became mandatory for the education of the Vietnamese elite.[8] To demonstrate that Li Thanh Tong did not view knowledge purely on a nationalistic level, the temple itself is dedicated to the great Chinese scholar Confucius.

---

[8] Murray, Geoffrey. *Culture Smart! Vietnam: The Essential Guide to Customs & Culture.* Pg. 30.

The entranceway to the Temple of Literature.⁷

The Temple of Literature was meant to be a focal point of enlightenment for the world. It celebrated genius minds, whether they happened to be Vietnamese or from somewhere else. Later Ly emperors were able to further bolster the civilization they ruled over by initiating reforms and intellectual innovations, as well as much-needed upgrades to infrastructure. For instance, the Ly dynasty created a dike system, which enabled a much more efficient practice of rice farming. There was also the utilization of a newly established court examination system, which was created to recruit eligible common people to high positions in government. This sort of recruitment to the civil service occurred every few years and was very important for the foundation of the Vietnamese civil structure.

Equally important was the establishment of a sound implementation of taxation. All governments need tax revenue in order to keep the government operating, and this ancient Vietnamese kingdom was no different. The taxes gleaned from the subject peoples kept the government afloat. In return, the government provided protection and civil services.

The Ly dynasty was known for a comparatively humane approach to governance. Chronicles record that punishments were sometimes reduced, prisoners could be granted amnesties, and officials were expected to avoid excessive cruelty. Women also enjoyed a more prominent role in public life than in many neighboring states. Noblewomen and members of the royal family could hold estates, oversee local administration, and in some cases manage the collection of taxes. While true equality of the sexes was far from realized, the Ly period retained a degree of gender balance inherited from Vietnam's older, indigenous traditions.

It was around this time that Buddhism began to gain greater prominence with the state government of the north, though it coexisted with other important philosophical and religious traditions. Vietnam found itself at a cultural crossroads, absorbing influences from multiple directions. From China came Confucianism, the philosophical system emphasizing social hierarchy, filial piety, and loyalty to both family and state, which became the foundation of the Vietnamese government and education. Buddhism, also originating from China and India, provided spiritual guidance and shaped popular religious life. Meanwhile, the Kingdom of Champa in the south professed a strong belief in Hinduism.

Vietnamese culture developed as a unique blend of these influences, with Confucianism dominating official governance and the educated elite and Buddhism permeating spiritual and religious practice among all classes. During this period, there was a constant interplay between these traditions in Vietnamese society, a dynamic that never completely disappeared but evolved over time. The influence of Champa's Hindu culture gradually diminished as Vietnamese territories expanded southward, though physical monuments erected by the Champa—such as the Cham towers—can still be seen throughout Vietnam today.

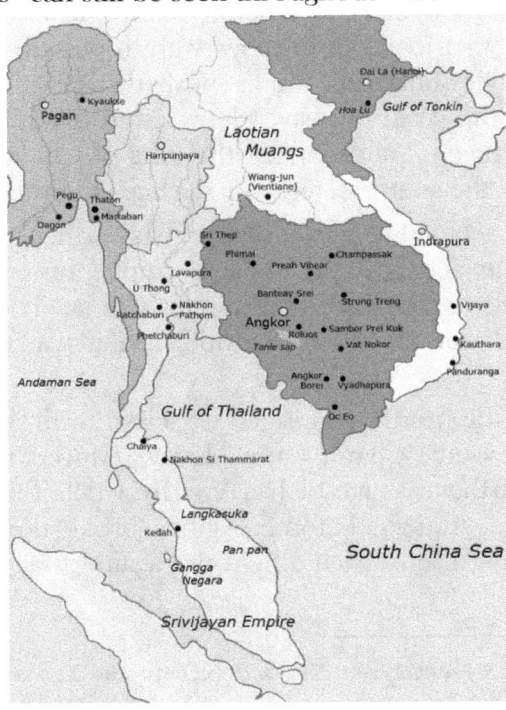

A map of Vietnam around 1000 CE.[a]

The entire landscape of Southeast Asia had changed considerably by 1000 CE. Vietnam's mighty neighbor to the north, China, had forged a new dynasty called the Song. The Song dynasty, although quite innovative and inventive, was in a weaker state militarily than the previous Tang dynasty. As such, it was much more cautious about military engagements.

This dynasty tended to pick and choose its battles and avoid conflict unless it was absolutely necessary. This granted Vietnam a freer hand since it was not under too much pressure on its northern frontier. However, this did not stop them from facing threats from the south, such as those from the Khmer Empire.[9]

The Khmer first launched an invasion of the region in 980 CE. Around 1080, the Khmers reached central Champa. Things then escalated quite seriously when Champa was laid siege to by the mighty Suryavarman II of the Khmer Empire in 1145. After a brief occupation, Suryavarman II's forces were pushed back to the south.

Northern Vietnam, in the meantime, would soon be beset with a new foe in the form of the Mongol Empire. The Mongols had managed to topple China's Song dynasty and began to look toward Vietnam. They poured into Dai Viet in 1258, but they were repulsed. They tried again in 1285 and 1288 but were again pushed back. These incursions occurred during the Tran dynasty, which lasted from 1225 to 1400. In 1307, Princess Huyen Tran married the king of Champa, which led to greater control of the southern territory during Tran rule.[10]

The Mongols seemed to finally realize that northern Vietnam was not worth the trouble and gave up their attempts. Instead, they became content just to focus on their holdings in China. The Mongols were ultimately kicked out of China in 1368, giving rise to China's Ming dynasty.

Dai Viet in the north continued to clash with the Kingdom of Champa to the south. Champa was slowly reduced to a vassal state, becoming a full tributary state of Dai Viet by 1312. This only lasted for roughly a decade, though, before relations broke down, and the two sides began warring against each other once again.

---

[9] Stuart-Fox, Martin. *A Short History of China and Southeast Asia: Tribute, Trade, and Influence.* 2003. Pg. 46.

[10] Murray, Geoffrey. *Culture Smart! Vietnam: The Essential Guide to Customs & Culture.* Pg. 34.

The endless wars served to bankrupt and utterly exhaust the Tran dynasty, which was ultimately cast to the side in 1400. By the end of the 14th century, the Tran dynasty, which had ruled Vietnam for more than 170 years, was in steep decline. Once celebrated for their victories over the Mongols, the Tran rulers had grown weak, indulgent, and increasingly out of touch with their people. Corruption spread through the court, the nobility lived in luxury, and the burden of taxes and forced labor fell heavily upon the common folk. It was in this troubled climate that a powerful nobleman named Ho Quy Ly rose to prominence.

Ho Quy Ly was no ordinary court official. He was ambitious, shrewd, and willing to take risks that others would not. Through marriage ties, he gained influence within the royal family itself. His daughter married into the Tran house, placing him ever closer to the throne. By the 1390s, he was effectively the most powerful man in the kingdom. Then, in 1399, Ho Quy Ly made his boldest move yet. With the emperor still a mere child, Ho orchestrated a coup d'etat. The boy emperor was forced to abdicate, and Ho Quy Ly installed his own son, Ho Han Thuong, as the new ruler. Though his son wore the crown, everyone understood who truly held the reins of power.

In 1400, Ho Quy Ly cast aside all pretense. He abolished the Tran dynasty altogether and declared the founding of a new royal line: the Ho dynasty. He even changed the name of the country from Dai Viet to Dai Ngu, a symbolic attempt to start afresh.

Ho was not only a usurper but also a reformer. He attempted sweeping changes, redistributing land from wealthy nobles and Buddhist temples. He also issued Vietnam's first paper money and expanded Confucian education as the new backbone of government service.

However, as radical as his reforms were, they did not win him lasting support. The powerful aristocracy resented losing land and influence. The Buddhist clergy bristled at his attempts to curb their privileges. To make matters worse, peasants were weary of war, taxes, and forced labor. Ho's heavy-handed style gave them little relief. Discontent festered across the kingdom.

This unrest did not go unnoticed by Vietnam's powerful neighbor to the north. The newly established Ming dynasty of China claimed that it would "restore" the Tran dynasty to its rightful place, but its true goal was conquest. In 1406, the Ming launched a full-scale invasion. By 1407, Ho Quy Ly and his son had been captured and taken in chains to China.

The Ho dynasty had lasted barely seven years. The Ming imposed direct rule over Vietnam, beginning two decades of harsh foreign occupation.[11] The Ming claimed that since there was no successor to the Tran dynasty, they would simply absorb northern Vietnam outright.

The Ming not only subdued the northern Vietnamese militarily, but they also attempted to subdue them culturally. They essentially sought to erase indigenous cultural identity in order to superimpose a Chinese one. The Chinese authorities banned Vietnamese books and replaced them with Chinese works of literature. Chinese enforcers sought to influence the everyday life of occupied Dai Ngu and even went as far as to impose Chinese fashion on the masses. Vietnamese women were made to wear Chinese clothes and to put up their hair in styles officially approved by the Chinese. Men likewise were forced to adhere to Chinese customs of dress.[12]

Almost as soon as the Ming dynasty imposed its direct rule over Vietnam, resistance began to smolder. The occupation quickly turned into a costly mistake for the Chinese court. Far from being a jewel in their crown, northern Vietnam became a constant drain on Ming resources, as the region demanded endless soldiers and supplies to put down rebellions. This was money and manpower the Ming could have used more wisely elsewhere.

No matter how hard the Ming tried to stamp out resistance, rebellion continued to boil beneath the surface. In 1418, a wealthy nobleman named Le Loi lit the spark that would become a wildfire. At first, he commanded little more than a ragtag group of rebels in the hills of Thanh Hoa. His early campaigns nearly ended in catastrophe. At one point, he was nearly captured by Ming forces. Capture would almost certainly have meant execution, which would have ended his rebellion. However, Le Loi survived, and with survival came hope.

By 1424, Le Loi's fortunes began to turn. That same year, the mighty Ming Yongle Emperor died, leaving Beijing temporarily distracted. Le Loi seized the opportunity. His rebel forces struck boldly at Ming positions, winning victories in Nghe An province and rallying more supporters to his cause.

---

[11] Stuart-Fox, Martin. *A Short History of China and Southeast Asia: Tribute, Trade, and Influence.* Pg. 81.
[12] Murray, Geoffrey. *Culture Smart! Vietnam: The Essential Guide to Customs & Culture.* Pg. 27.

From that point forward, momentum was on the rebels' side. By 1426, Le Loi's armies had swept across the Red River Delta, capturing fortress after fortress and even laying siege to Dong Quan, the Ming stronghold that would later become Hanoi. Vietnam was on the cusp of freedom, and the Chinese occupiers were beginning to realize their hold on the land was slipping away.[13]

The Ming attempted to send reinforcements to salvage their campaign, but it was too late. In 1427, Le Loi's forces annihilated a large Chinese relief army at Chi Lang and Xuong Giang, breaking the last hope of restoring Ming control. By early 1428, the exhausted occupiers finally withdrew, and Vietnam was free once again.

Le Loi's rebellion had begun with scattered ambushes and guerrilla strikes, but by its climax, it had swelled into a powerful army that never gave the Chinese a moment's peace. Even with their superior numbers, the Ming could not endure the relentless hit-and-run attacks, the constant uprisings, and the steady erosion of their garrisons. In the end, Chinese officials decided it was wiser to cut their losses than bleed endlessly for a land that refused to submit.

With the Ming gone, Le Loi declared himself emperor, taking the reign name Le Thai To. He founded the Later Le dynasty in 1428. This dynasty would endure, in one form or another, until 1789. By 1431, Ming China formally recognized the new dynasty, though the sting of their defeat in Vietnam was still fresh.

The year 1471 marked a decisive turning point in Vietnamese history. Under Emperor Le Thanh Tong, the armies of northern Vietnam launched a massive campaign against the Kingdom of Champa. The Vietnamese forces stormed Vijaya, Champa's capital, in a brutal war of conquest that left the kingdom shattered. Contemporary accounts speak of staggering losses. They say some sixty thousand Cham people were killed, while another thirty thousand were taken as prisoners of war.

With this crushing blow, much of central and southern Vietnam was absorbed into a greater Vietnamese state. Champa, once a powerful kingdom along the central coast, was reduced to a shadow of its former self, confined to the far south. From this moment forward, Vietnam's long march southward—the Nam tien—accelerated, reshaping the map of Southeast Asia.

---

[13] Stuart-Fox, Martin. *A Short History of China and Southeast Asia: Tribute, Trade, and Influence*. Pg. 90.

DAI VIET EMPIRE (VIETNAM) DURING THE REIGN OF EMPEROR LÊ THÁNH TÔNG, 1480

Dai Viet during Le Thanh Tong's rule.*

The world was changing as it entered the Age of Exploration. This exploration was driven by profit and trade just as much as curiosity. It was kick-started when Islamic forces toppled the capital of the Byzantine Empire, Constantinople, which had long been a major trading hub on the Silk Road, in 1453. Byzantium linked the East and the West, but after the Islamic Turks seized Constantinople, the Silk Road was largely blocked to European traders. Over the next few decades, Middle Eastern merchants and their Venetian associates began to charge extraordinarily high prices on trade goods from the East. If you wanted any sort of exotic spices from the East, you would have to pay a small fortune to get them.

Not only did this upset fine connoisseurs of spices, but the imbalanced trade also weakened Western economies. As such, the Europeans began to consider finding an alternate trade route. Spain and Portugal led the charge. Portugal literally made major waves when it circumnavigated the southern tip of Africa in 1488. Ten years later, the Portuguese landed in India. This was a monumental event, akin to landing on the moon. It shocked the world. Now, the Portuguese had cut out the middleman and could obtain spices and other precious commodities directly from the source, thereby destroying the monopoly that had made Middle Eastern power brokers so rich and powerful.

This was really part of a larger geopolitical sort of medieval "Cold War" between Western Christian European and Middle Eastern Muslim powers. The success of the Portuguese was a game-changer. It would also change the game quite a bit in Southeast Asia and eventually Vietnam.

The Portuguese seized the strategic port city of Malacca (located in modern-day Malaysia) in 1511. This gave them a significant foothold in Southeast Asia and a forward base for further exploration. The first Portuguese sailors arrived on Vietnamese shores in 1516.[14] They steadily increased their presence over the years.

Vietnam in the early 16th century was torn apart by civil war. In 1527, the Mac family had usurped the throne from the Later Le dynasty. Le loyalists, backed by the powerful Trinh and Nguyen families, restored a rival Le emperor in 1533, creating two competing courts. This ongoing conflict weakened Vietnam considerably.

It was into this divided kingdom that European traders first arrived. By the 1550s, the Portuguese had reached the Viet-

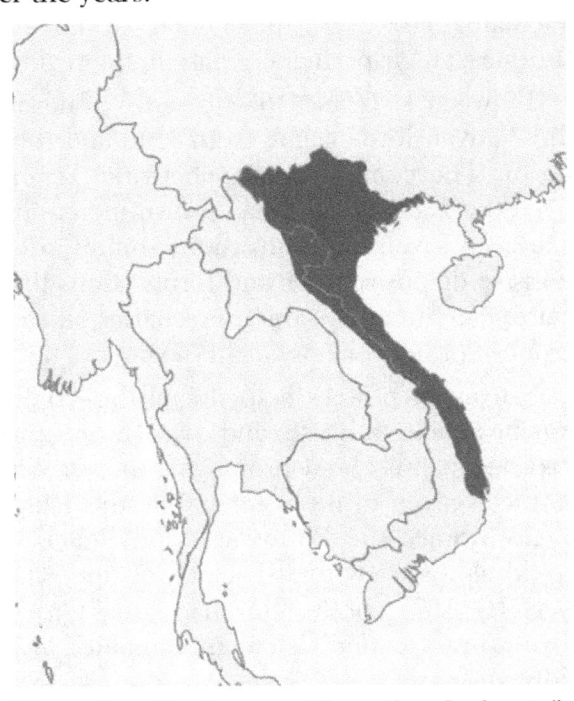

The northern Mac dynasty and the southern Le dynasty.[10]

---

[14] Stuart-Fox, Martin. *A Short History of China and Southeast Asia: Tribute, Trade, and Influence.* Pg. 95.

namese harbor of Faifo (near modern-day Da Nang). The Portuguese had set up another base of operations in Macao in southern China in 1557. They began referring to Vietnam as Cochinchina. They apparently did so for a couple of reasons. First, they mispronounced the Chinese term for Vietnam, which was Jiaozhi ("Giao Chi"). The Portuguese rendered this term as "Cauchi." Then, in a bid to make sure no Portuguese sailor confused India with the region, they slapped the word China at the end of it and began calling the region Cochinchina. The fact that Vietnam and surrounding regions, such as Laos and Cambodia, would later become known as Indochina (and, after the French ran roughshod through the region, as French Indochina) can be traced back to this appellation.[15]

In the mid-17th century, the Portuguese were being supplanted by their rivals, the Dutch. Although the Portuguese had beaten the Dutch in exploring the great expanses of Asia, the Dutch had caught up with them by the 1600s and began to make their influence known as far afield as Vietnam. However, the Dutch would make the Spice Islands of Indonesia their permanent base in the region.

Between 1627 and 1672, a series of devastating wars erupted between the Nguyen lords ruling from Hue and the Trinh lords controlling the north. The conflict began when the Trinh demanded full submission from the Nguyen, who had grown increasingly independent. The Trinh launched seven major invasions southward, but the Nguyen constructed massive defensive walls and fortifications that held firm. Both sides used European firearms and mercenaries, turning Vietnam into a proving ground for new military technologies.

European powers helped fuel this conflict by arming both sides. It was profitable to do so, and many unscrupulous European arms dealers had no qualms about prolonging the war. The Portuguese rendered aid to the Nguyen in the south, while the Dutch aided the northern Trinh faction. Since the Portuguese and Dutch were rivals at the time, one could almost view their backing of opposite factions as a kind of proxy war. By 1672, both sides had fought to exhaustion, and though the formal wars ended, Vietnam remained divided between the two rival domains.

---

[15] Karnow, Stanley. *Vietnam: A History*. Pg. 70.

After the wars subsided, the Nguyen consolidated their power in the south, expanding Vietnamese territory southward into the Mekong Delta and transforming Hue into a magnificent capital city. The Nguyen court attracted scholars and artists, sponsored Confucian academies, and patronized literature and the arts, creating a vibrant cultural center that blended Vietnamese, Chinese, and indigenous Southeast Asian traditions.

It was into this divided but culturally vibrant Vietnam that French intervention began. In 1674, French explorers set up shop at their settlement of Pondicherry on the eastern shores of India. It was from here that the French would slowly make inroads into the rest of Vietnam.

It would take some time, though. Throughout the 1700s, Vietnam remained fiercely independent, even though the Nguyen and Trinh domains often skirmished against each other.

An 18th-century Vietnamese cross.[11]

Catholic French missionaries had been making inroads into Vietnam as well. Their efforts can be traced back to 1658, when French church officials formed the Paris Foreign Missions Society, a group dedicated to converting the peoples of Asia. By 1664, they had opened their seminary in Paris to prepare missionaries for their work abroad.[16] Inroads made in the 17th century and even the 18th century were initially rather modest and slow-going. However, clearing the way for the French was the lasting legacy of the Portuguese. Portuguese Jesuit missionaries were the first to apply the Latin script to the Vietnamese language in the 17th century. Working with local converts, they began adapting it into a

---

[16] Karnow, Stanley. *Vietnam: A History*. Pg. 73.

form that could capture the tones and sounds of Vietnamese, laying the groundwork for what would later be known as "chu Quoc Ngu." Vietnam is unique among East Asian nations since it is the only country that has swapped indigenous characters entirely for a Latin script.

    At any rate, now that the Vietnamese knew their Latin ABCs, the door was open for French missionaries, philosophers, political tyrants, and other ideologues to start plying their trade in earnest.

Chapter 5: French Conquest of Vietnam

"Never has an era seen such sadness, never a year more anguish. Above me, I fear the edicts of heaven. Below, the tribulations of the people trouble my days and nights. Deep in my heart, I tremble and blush, finding neither words nor actions to help my subjects. Alone, I am speechless. My pulse is feeble, my body pale and thin, my beard and hair white. Though not yet forty, I have already reached old age, so that I lack the strength to pay homage to my ancestors every morning and evening."

-*Vietnamese Emperor Tu Doc*[17]

In 1787, a French bishop by the name of Pierre Joseph Georges Pigneau de Behaine arrived at the court of King Louis and Queen Marie Antoinette on a crucial diplomatic mission. He had spent years as a missionary in Cochinchina and had come to France with a specific purpose: to secure military aid for his embattled ally, Prince Nguyen Phuc Anh. Assisting him with this diplomatic endeavor was a very special guest: Nguyen Phuc Canh.

Nguyen Phuc Canh was seven years old at the time. He was a precocious Vietnamese child and the crown prince, the eldest son of Vietnamese Prince Nguyen Phuc Anh, who would later become

---

[17] Karnow, Stanley. *Vietnam: A History.* Pg. 91.

Emperor Gia Long.[18] Pigneau de Behaine had first become acquainted with Nguyen Phuc Anh during his years as a missionary in the region.

Back then, thanks to the Portuguese, Europeans referred to the region as Cochinchina. As such, Behaine and his colleagues referred to Prince Anh, as well as his son, Prince Canh, as princes of Cochinchina.

Cochinchina was a strange, exotic, and mysterious place for most of the denizens of France at the time. Any word from this faraway land was always greeted with great interest. Any potential missionary bold enough to head into these uncharted waters typically did not know what they would be getting into upon their arrival.

But how did this young Vietnamese prince end up at the French court, thousands of miles from home? To understand this, one must go back sixteen years to 1771, when Prince Nguyen Phuc Anh's world began to fall apart.

The Tay Son Rebellion erupted in the vicinity of the Tay Son Mountains. The rebellion was an all-out insurrection that was launched in 1771 against the Nguyen lords, who ruled southern Vietnam from their base at Hue. The Tay Son Brothers—Nguyen Hue, Nguyen Nhac, and Nguyen Lu—led a major populist uprising fueled by crushing tax burdens, rampant corruption among Nguyen officials, and widespread regional instability. They were referred to as the "Tay Son Brothers" because they hailed from the Vietnamese town of Tay Son.

During the course of their rebellion, the Tay Son Brothers were able to tap into the deep dissatisfaction among the lower classes and use it to their advantage. Chief among the complaints that galvanized the masses to revolt was excessive taxation. Taxation has been known to ruffle feathers in just about every era and in just about every part of the globe—and it was no different for Vietnam. The revolt gained steam, transforming into a populist movement geared toward overthrowing the Nguyen lords themselves.

The rebels cobbled together their own army, and by 1775, they had seized the southern city of Saigon. Further demonstrating the populist nature of this revolt, those in charge of it instituted popular reforms, such as land redistribution and reforms aimed at the agricultural sector and the better execution of taxation.[19]

---

[18] Karnow, Stanley. *Vietnam: A History.* Pg. 68.
[19] Karnow, Stanley. *Vietnam: A History.* Pg. 74.

By 1777, the Tay Son forces had dealt the Nguyen lords a devastating blow. They stormed the Nguyen stronghold and killed many members of the royal family. Prince Nguyen Phuc Anh barely escaped with his life. For the next decade, he would live as a fugitive, constantly on the run from Tay Son forces. He controlled almost no territory, having been reduced from a powerful lord to a desperate refugee.

It was during these dark days that the hunted and hounded Prince Nguyen Phuc Anh sought refuge with Pierre Pigneau de Behaine. The French bishop saw an opportunity and convinced the prince to allow him to travel to France to request that the French government intervene on his behalf. As part of this diplomatic strategy, Pigneau persuaded Nguyen Phuc Anh to send his own son, the young Prince Nguyen Phuc Canh, to accompany him to the French court. The presence of the charming young prince would make the mission far more compelling.

This brings us back to 1787 and the young prince's dramatic appearance before King Louis XVI and Queen Marie Antoinette. There were, from the very beginning, questions about whether Prince Nguyen Phuc Anh, who was still a refugee at the time, had the legitimate authority to make treaties on behalf of Vietnam since the Tay Son rebels controlled most of the country. Nevertheless, Pigneau de Behaine signed the Treaty of Versailles on November 28th, 1787, on behalf of Prince Nguyen Phuc Anh, promising French military aid in exchange for territorial concessions and trade privileges.

Nguyen Phuc Canh caused quite a stir at the palace of King Louis XVI. Queen Marie Antoinette was particularly fond of the child and reportedly arranged for him to spend time with her son, France's own crown prince (commonly referred to as the Dauphin). France was, of course, going through a great transition during those days. It was the eve of the French Revolution, which would ultimately break out on May 5th, 1789.

The turmoil of the French Revolution would ultimately lead to Queen Marie Antoinette and her husband, King Louis XVI, losing their heads. The guillotine began slamming down upon anyone viewed as being against the currents of the French Revolution. As France descended into chaos, the treaty signed on behalf of Prince Nguyen Phuc Anh was abandoned. The French government, facing financial ruin and political upheaval, never sent the promised military aid.

However, Pigneau de Behaine was not deterred. Unable to secure official French support, he raised private funds and recruited French mercenaries on his own. He returned to Vietnam with modern weapons, warships, and military advisers. With this crucial assistance, Prince Nguyen Phuc Anh began his comeback.

Through the 1790s, equipped with European military technology and French tactical expertise, Prince Nguyen Phuc Anh gradually reconquered southern Vietnam. In 1799, his forces recaptured Saigon. By 1801, he had defeated the last Tay Son emperor and conquered northern Vietnam, unifying the country for the first time in centuries.

Tragically, Prince Nguyen Phuc Canh did not live to see his father's victory. The young man who had charmed the French court as a child died on March 20th, 1801, at the age of twenty-one. This opened up the question of succession. After considerable internal debate, Nguyen Phuc Anh eventually designated Canh's younger brother, Nguyen Phuc Dam, to be his heir.

In 1802, Prince Nguyen Phuc Anh finally ascended to the throne as emperor, calling himself Emperor Gia Long. This kick-started the Nguyen dynasty—the last royal dynasty of Vietnam. Two years later, in 1804, he officially adopted the name Vietnam for his unified kingdom.

The French Revolution would eventually result in the placement of a previously obscure general, Napoleon Bonaparte, at the very top of the French hierarchy. Dubbing himself an emperor, Napoleon would wage wars over the next couple of decades. The subsequent Napoleonic Wars would last until 1815, and it would take France another few decades to recover. Ironically, Napoleon's nephew,

Emperor Gia Long.[13]

Napoleon Bonaparte III, would explore the prospect of greater French influence in Vietnam in earnest.

The Nguyen dynasty practiced a limited form of openness with Europeans. For instance, it was open to Catholic missionaries, who had already established a strong foothold in the region. His successor, Nguyen Phuc Dam, however, would not be quite so tolerant.

Emperor Gia Long died in 1819, and he had designated Nguyen Phuc Dam as his successor. Phuc Dam, who became Emperor Minh Mang, fell into the conservative wing of Vietnamese politics during this era, which was wary of foreign encroachment and especially the spread of Christianity. It was feared that Christianity was diluting Vietnam's Confucian traditions, especially by placing spiritual authority in a foreign pope rather than the Vietnamese emperor and by undermining the hierarchical social order upon which Vietnamese governance depended.

A portrait of Minh Mang.[18]

Minh Mang was also astute enough to read the writing on the wall, as he seemed to sense that granting further concessions to the French and the missionaries would only lead them to ask for more. His attempts to centralize power and reduce regional autonomy sparked resistance among local elites, and when revolts broke out in the early 1830s, some Christian communities joined the rebels in hopes of gaining religious freedom. Minh Mang suspected Catholic priests had instigated these uprisings, and he cracked down on them harshly. The worst of his crackdowns occurred in 1833 when a French priest, Francois-Isidore Gagelin, was arrested and executed on the orders of Minh Mang. He was brutally strangled to death on October 17th, 1833.

The many Catholic martyrs slain during the persecutions in Vietnam.[14]

Minh Mang not only demonstrated his contempt for Christianity but also his fearful paranoia toward what he considered to be the strange ideas of Christianity. He actually had the priest's dead body exhumed after three days so that he could make sure that he had not been resurrected. Minh Mang had apparently read up on Christianity enough to know that Jesus was said to have been resurrected on the third day, and he feared that the priest just might do the same.

After news of this horrid episode reached France, the French were understandably outraged. But they were not yet in a position to do anything about it. It was not until almost a decade later, in 1842, when the British opened the doors of China after the First Opium War, that the French began to consider their own position in Asia. Their connections in Vietnam naturally came to mind.

It was also on the elderly Minh Mang's mind too. His animosity had cooled at this point, giving rise to pragmatic reason. Alarmed by the ease with which the British had defeated the juggernaut to the north (China), Minh Mang began to think it might be prudent to negotiate. He even went as far as to dispatch a couple of emissaries to the French court to see what kind of deal might be worked out. This was very wise of the Vietnamese ruler. Rather than wait and see what happened when it came to the European dash for colonial territory, he decided to beat the French to the punch by directly initiating talks with them in advance.

With the outrage of the priest who had been executed several years prior still fresh in the minds of the French, these emissaries were largely given the cold shoulder. As it turns out, it did not really matter too much because Minh Mang died shortly after this aborted olive branch with the French had been attempted. His successor, Emperor Thieu Tri, reversed course and began to once again shun any relations with France.

This set Vietnam on a path toward deeper conflict with France. In 1843, Admiral Cecille's fleet anchored in Vietnamese waters with the purpose of protecting French interests and securing the release of imprisoned Catholic missionaries. For Emperor Thieu Tri, this was an ominous sign. French ships could respond instantly if tensions escalated. While France was not yet openly committed to conquest, Thieu Tri recognized that any misstep could be seized upon as a pretext for armed intervention. His suspicion only deepened when some Catholic clergy were accused of meddling in Vietnamese politics. Yet, any decisive move against them risked provoking exactly the kind of military confrontation he wished to avoid.

In 1845, Emperor Thieu Tri ordered the arrest of French missionary Dominique Lefebvre for returning to Vietnam illegally and allegedly meddling in political affairs. The emperor initially sentenced him to death, which was the usual penalty for such an offense, but he commuted the sentence to imprisonment to avoid provoking France. Even from his cell, Lefebvre managed to contact a visiting foreign ship in port. That vessel turned out not to be French but the American frigate USS *Constitution*. Its commander, John Percival, demanded Lefebvre's release and an end to the persecution of Christians. Reluctantly, Thieu Tri gave in and allowed the missionary to depart.

Lefebvre soon slipped back into Vietnam and was arrested again in 1847. This time, the French decided to act. Two French warships anchored at Tourane in April, demanding his release and religious freedom for Catholics. Talks quickly soured, and on April 15th, the French fleet opened fire, destroying much of the Vietnamese navy, which was anchored, and killing hundreds. Having made their point, the ships withdrew. Later that year, Emperor Thieu Tri died and was succeeded by Tu Duc, who would inherit the deepening crisis in Vietnam's relations with France.[20]

Tu Duc reversed course once again as it pertained to Vietnam's policy toward outsiders. Seeing outside influence as the cause of all of Vietnam's problems, he closed—or at least attempted to close—the door to outside contact. He also ramped up persecution of Christians, going as far as to issue an anti-Christian edict in 1848, giving the French the pretext they so desperately craved.

Tu Duc was caught in an impossible dilemma. Granting concessions to foreigners would invite further demands and undermine his authority, but resistance would provoke European military intervention. He chose to prioritize internal stability and Confucian order, gambling that a hardline stance might discourage French ambitions—a calculation that would prove disastrously wrong.

The actual persecution of Christians was nothing that could be glossed over. In his contempt and hatred of the faith, Emperor Tu Duc went as far as to have converted Vietnamese Christians branded on the cheek with the words *ta dao*, which translates roughly as "infidel." He was essentially slapping an easily recognizable "dunce cap" on their

---

[20] Karnow, Stanley. *Vietnam: A History*. Pg. 81.

heads, ensuring they would be derided, mistreated, and humiliated wherever they went just because they were Christians. This practice echoed an older Vietnamese custom in which criminals or even the children of criminals were branded on the face to mark them as lesser beings. These Christians were not slaves, but they were treated in much the same way. They were denied the dignity normally afforded to members of a civil society. So, yes, although the French had been desperately seeking a pretext to wage a war of conquest and colonization, the persecution of Christians was very real.

In 1848, the nephew of the long-deposed and since-deceased Napoleon Bonaparte, Napoleon III, came to power in France. Initially, he was a democratically elected president meant to serve for a limited term that was set to expire in 1852. This all changed when Napoleon III launched a coup just prior to the end of his term in December of 1851. This coup resulted in him being hailed as an autocratic leader. He was the new emperor of France.

Interestingly enough, this coup was strongly supported by a certain faction of French Catholics, so the persecuted Catholics in Vietnam were suddenly some of Napoleon III's best constituents. His wife Eugenie, who hailed from staunchly Catholic Spain, is also believed to have had a heavy influence on her husband Napoleon III's decisions.[21]

Napoleon III realized that the best pretext for war is something that can make one look less like a belligerent bully and more like an avenging hero. Rather than waging unwarranted aggression, Napoleon III could try to cover up France's vainglorious ambition under the cloak of protecting the persecuted Christian minority. It was not long before Napoleon III ordered a punitive expedition to Vietnam to teach Emperor Tu Duc a lesson.[22] However, he could not move against Vietnam in full force until his entanglements in Europe had been taken care of.

At the time, France was aligned with England and had to deal with the Crimean War, which was being waged against Russia on behalf of the Ottoman Empire. This in itself was a major shift in geopolitics since the Turks, who had shocked Christendom by toppling Constantinople, were now in an open alliance with Western European Christian nations

---

[21] Karnow, Stanley. *Vietnam: A History.* Pg. 84.
[22] Karnow, Stanley. *Vietnam: A History.* Pg. 84.

against Russia. Ironically, part of Russia's pretext for war against the Ottomans (as was the case on more than a few occasions) was that the Ottomans were allegedly mistreating Christians in the Balkans. Yes, even as France was getting ready to ramp up aggression against Vietnam on the pretext of rescuing persecuted Christians, they were helping the Ottomans beat back the Russians, who were allegedly trying to do the exact same thing.

There was another wrinkle in this complex web of events since the French were Catholic and the Russians were Orthodox. The two powers clashed over religious influence in Palestine, which at that time was under the authority of the Ottoman Turks. France pressed for Catholic primacy at the holy sites, while Russia demanded that preference be given to the Orthodox faith. This quarrel over sacred ground, coupled with larger strategic rivalries, was one of the sparks that helped ignite the Crimean War. With France's attention drawn to this European conflict, which lasted between 1853 and 1856, and to its disputes with the Russians and the Ottomans, only limited energy could be directed toward aggression in Vietnam—at least for now.

In 1856, Paris authorized a limited naval demonstration against Vietnam. This was an exercise in classic gunboat diplomacy. The French squadron was ordered to make for Tourane (modern-day Da Nang) to demand an audience with Emperor Tu Duc. The aim was to force him to grant concessions, including the opening of Tourane as a French-controlled port, which Paris framed as "indemnity" for past affronts.

The fleet arrived that September and anchored in the harbor. For days, emissaries delivered demands that the Vietnamese court firmly rejected. Frustrated, the French ships opened fire, battering several coastal defenses before marines landed to briefly seize a nearby fortification. This was a punitive raid, not a full occupation. The French forces were small in number and could not hold the territory. After what they considered a suitable display of force, they withdrew to the Portuguese enclave of Macao to regroup.

Back in Paris, officials debated how far to take the matter. Some even dredged up the long-defunct 1787 Treaty of Versailles, which had been signed decades earlier between Nguyen Anh and Louis XVI, though it was quickly agreed that the document had no legal weight. Still, the idea of "teaching the Vietnamese a lesson" was appealing to those who wanted a colonial foothold in Southeast Asia.

Over the next year, the French strategy took shape. The Paris government, now with Spanish cooperation—Spain had its own grievances over persecution of Catholic missionaries—began to plan a large-scale punitive expedition. This joint Franco-Spanish force would be far more substantial than the 1856 detachment, numbering about three thousand troops, including marines, artillery, and Filipino auxiliaries. The aim was clear. They were to seize and hold Tourane as a permanent base and then force open Vietnam's ports through sustained military pressure.

The fleet showed up at Tourane on August 31st, 1858, and the attack began the very next day. Needless to say, this large fleet was able to quickly overwhelm the defenses of Tourane. However, after landing and establishing a foothold, the French began to suffer casualties almost immediately. This was not so much from fighting but more due to exhaustion from the scorching heat and the outbreak of tropical diseases, such as dysentery and cholera. The French and their allies were simply not prepared for what awaited them.[23]

For one thing, they wore cumbersome, heavy uniforms that did not fare well in the hot, tropical sun. Men passed out from heat stroke and battled dysentery and cholera.[24] There was also the problem of Vietnam's wet terrain, which required boats to travel up and down rivers. The expedition was not prepared for this contingency either, so the men did not have suitable watercraft to traverse the many rivers of Vietnam.

Conditions would only grow worse as summer turned into fall, as the monsoon rains hit, making the terrain a nearly untraversable muddy mess. Keep in mind that the Vietnamese knew their terrain and the hardships it presented better than anyone. They had spent many centuries making full use of it to repel enemies ranging from the Chinese to the Mongolians to the Champa, and they were more than likely preparing a similar long-term strategy to deal with the French.

At any rate, the invaders were in for a tough slog through hot and humid conditions in the Southeast Asian environment of Vietnam. The first real territorial gain came several months later, in February of 1859, when the fleet moved farther south and captured the site of modern-day Ho Chi Minh City; it was called Gia Dinh at the time.

---

[23] Karnow, Stanley. *Vietnam: A History.* Pg. 87.
[24] Karnow, Stanley. *Vietnam: A History.* Pg. 87.

French troops then laid siege to Saigon, assaulting the city in February of 1859. The French were dismayed to find that even after taking the city, the Vietnamese were an intractable foe. Their ambush-style attacks in the countryside allowed them to maintain a constant state of vigilance. The French, despite their superior arms, were being repeatedly hit from all sides. If they did not make serious gains soon, they risked losing everything they had gained.

French warships attacking Saigon.[14]

French commander Charles Rigault de Genouilly left a small, fortified garrison under Captain Bernard Jaureguiberry while withdrawing the main bulk of French forces back to Tourane. The situation in Tourane was not much better, with French forces facing the same guerrilla warfare tactics while also suffering from the heat and tropical illnesses. By the summer of 1859, the situation seemed absolutely dire.[25]

Figuring it might be a good time to negotiate (before his position weakened any further), Rigault de Genouilly attempted to parley with Vietnamese Emperor Tu Duc. Emperor Tu Duc must have believed that he had the upper hand since he refused to even consider negotiations. Rigault de Genouilly, facing a campaign that was dragging on without a decisive victory and meeting resistance both in Vietnam and in Paris, eventually resigned later that year and returned to France.

---

[25] Karnow, Stanley. *Vietnam: A History.* Pg. 88.

He would be succeeded by Admiral Leonard Victor Joseph Charner. Charner was a much more serious man as it pertained to achieving a strategic victory in Vietnam. Rather than a punitive expedition, the French were now determined to establish a permanent colonial presence. In early 1861, Charner arrived with several thousand troops and fought his way back to Saigon, securing the city by February 1861. This time around, the French were playing for keeps.

After pushing far into the Mekong Delta and decimating a large number of Vietnamese troops, Emperor Tu Doc was finally pressured to enter into a peace treaty. This resulted in the Saigon Treaty of 1862, which granted the French not only Saigon but also three other provinces in the south, along with control of Poulo Condor Island. Almost as an afterthought (even though it was ostensibly the main reason for the war), the French won the concession of allowing Catholic missionaries to preach and spread the gospel without any interference from the Vietnamese government.

Emperor Tu Doc was suddenly very amenable to French demands. What caused this about-face? Besides the threat of French arms, the real threat that the French posed was the fact that after taking over the Mekong Delta, they had put a stranglehold on rice production, which was very prevalent in the south. Emperor Tu Doc was faced with the prospect of his people starving if he did not come to terms with the French. Since starving soldiers would not be much use on the battlefield, he decided it was time to cut his losses and deal with his foes.

Unfortunately for him and the rest of the Vietnamese, this would not be a one-off. Soon, the French would demand even more. Interestingly, Napoleon III, while initially supportive of expanding French influence in Vietnam, remained wary of the costs of maintaining a large overseas presence. He was not looking to abandon Cochinchina, but he also had no interest in overextending French commitments without any clear benefits. For his part, Emperor Tu Doc made several overtures to limit French control, even floating the idea that France could restrict itself to influence rather than outright annexation of southern provinces. However, these suggestions were quietly rebuffed in Paris.

The fall of Napoleon III in 1870, which was brought on by the disastrous Franco-Prussian War, left the question of Vietnam's future in the hands of the new French Third Republic. At first, its leaders were hesitant to pursue costly colonial adventures. However, as the years went on, commercial ambitions, strategic calculations, and missionary lobbying gradually pushed France back toward expansion. By the early 1880s, this change in attitude had become unmistakable.

In 1882, French forces under Henri Riviere seized Hanoi, marking the start of a more aggressive push into northern Vietnam. The following year, Emperor Tu Doc died, leaving his country politically unstable and vulnerable. Over the next several years, France steadily expanded its holdings, securing Tonkin and extending control into Laos and Cambodia. In 1887, these acquisitions were formally consolidated into the "Indochinese Union," more commonly known at the time as French Indochina.

French officers and Tonkinese riflemen.[16]

Chapter 6: The Colonial Rule of French Indochina

"Don't you remember your history? The last time the Chinese came, they stayed a thousand years. The French are foreigners. They are weak. Colonialism is dying. The [French are] finished in Asia. But if the Chinese stay now, they will never go. As for me, I prefer to sniff French crap for five years than eat Chinese crap for the rest of my life."

-Ho Chi Minh[26]

Although France had control of Vietnam by the late 1800s, there were still pockets of resistance to be found. Up in the mountainous regions of Vietnam's far north, a rebel by the name of Hoang Hoa Tham staged cunning hit-and-run attacks against French forces until 1911.

As volatile as things were, the French quickly understood that in order to have any sense of peace and stability, they had to win over (at least some) of the hearts and minds of the people that they were administering over. The easiest constituency to win over was those Vietnamese who had already converted to Catholicism. For them, the French, as crude as they might be at times, still saved them from the religious persecution of the previous Vietnamese government. They could now practice their religion in peace, and they did not have to worry about having terrible epithets burned onto their faces in an effort

---

[26] Karnow, Stanley. *Vietnam: A History.* Pg. 169.

of systematic stigmatization. These Vietnamese at least had something to be happy about, and the French were wise enough to try to cultivate an alliance with them.

Old attitudes die hard. And as Catholic communities became more entangled with French administrators, suspicions only deepened. Many non-Catholic Vietnamese looked at Catholic collaborators with narrowed eyes. They might not have had the word "traitor" branded on their cheeks, but for some, that's exactly what they were.

In a few key regions, French officials leaned heavily on trusted Catholic allies, not just for translation or governance but also sometimes for intelligence. Whispers of rebellion, names of dissidents, movements in the countryside occasionally reached French ears. And when Catholic landowners were seen profiting from land redistribution or seizing property once held by others, resentment flared.

The result was a widening divide. There was a growing class of Catholic Vietnamese with ties to the colonial machine and a swelling population of landless peasants and sidelined villagers. The French, of course, saw opportunity. Every empire needs loyal locals, and Catholic France, seeing its own reflection in Vietnam's Christian minority, found its favorites.

This great rift that had been carved into Vietnamese society would have long-lasting repercussions, and the issue of land ownership would take center stage when the communists came to prominence. Communism would arrive in Vietnam in the following decades, introduced by Vietnamese nationalists like Ho Chi Minh, who had studied Marxist theory abroad. The promise of land redistribution would prove particularly appealing to the landless peasants created by French colonial policies, and by the 1940s, communists would become the leading force in Vietnam's independence struggle.

The French instituted sweeping changes to Vietnamese society. Prior to the colonial takeover, Vietnam had been organized around a rigid landlord-based hierarchy. The French disrupted this old order by replacing it with an administrative system modeled after their own—one that still had strict classes but introduced new avenues for advancement for those who aligned themselves with the colonial regime. While these opportunities were reserved for a small fraction of the population, they created a new class of Vietnamese who could navigate both traditional and French systems.

The French also expanded access to education—albeit to a select few—and promoted French as the language of administration and scholarship. Ironically, this effort helped produce a generation of educated Vietnamese who would later challenge colonial rule. These men and women studied French republican ideals, the works of Karl Marx, and other currents of modern political thought, alongside the Confucian classics of their own heritage. From this small but determined group emerged a modern Vietnamese intelligentsia. They were shaped under the very institutions of French imperialism, yet they became increasingly committed to bringing that same imperial order to an end.

Not everyone was calling for an all-out revolution. Some were just voicing their general displeasure and asking for reform. Not all colonies, after all, ditched their colonizer through bloody revolts. Some did so through reform. Even though the United States was born out of the Revolutionary War, Canadians shook off the British through a gradual process of reform. India, likewise, could be said to have followed a similar pattern.

One real game-changer in the independence movement came in 1904 with the appearance of *Van Minh Tan Hoc Sach* ("The Strategy of Civilization and New Learning"). This pamphlet pulled no punches, pointing out that Vietnam had fallen behind much of the rest of the world and could no longer cling to old habits if it wanted to survive. It called for modern schools, new ideas, and a willingness to learn from other nations. It was a wake-up call that struck a chord with a rising generation of reform-minded Vietnamese.

The pamphlet made the pragmatic point that Vietnam had already been eclipsed by other regional powers. Japan, for example, rapidly industrialized in the late 1800s. By the 1900s, it had become one of the leading nation-states on the planet. The writer of this text believed that Vietnam needed the same kind of revolutionary reforms in order to succeed and argued that the current French colonial system was stifling the process.

Those who advocated for reform wished to establish a republic in which the interests of the Vietnamese people could best be represented. Not everyone was reform-minded, though, and more radical revolutionaries emerged during this period. In particular, there was the so-called "Travel to the East" or Dong Du movement. This movement looked toward the success story of industrialized Japan and advocated that the Vietnamese should head to Japan to better learn how to modernize so that they could develop into a generation equipped to forcefully overthrow the French. It is ironic that this generation of Vietnamese youth would look toward Japan as their salvation when Japan would later invade and brutally occupy Vietnam.

The French soon became wary of both the revolutionaries and the reformers. They took steps to minimize this radical influence on Vietnam (or as they called it, French Indochina). The French set up their own form of internal intelligence and began to try to break up these groups of Vietnamese activists. This led to many arrests and even deportations. However, if the French wanted to completely destroy the intelligentsia they had helped create, it was too late. They would have had to shut down the schools, burn all the books, and erase the memories of former students. The reform- and revolutionary-minded had already made their minds up.

Exacerbating this problem even further was the fact that even though the Vietnamese youth were able to obtain an education if they so desired, the French had put a stranglehold on advancement. The Vietnamese could get lower-level jobs in the civil service, but there was a glass ceiling that they were not allowed to penetrate. Any position with any real authority was reserved for the French.

The French had found themselves caught in a trap that has been quite common to many authoritarian regimes with a restless populace. They often shifted between harsh austerity and liberal allowance. For instance, the Russian tsars of the late 1800s and early 1900s enacted reforms to appease an increasingly agitated public and then crack down on the very freedoms they had allowed.

The French did the same thing in French Indochina. It was in this dizzying back and forth of regulations that a young Ho Chi Minh grew up. The future communist leader of North Vietnam was born in 1890. He was actually born in central Vietnam, a region known to have birthed many of Vietnam's leaders. He came of age during the early 1900s when the reform movement was first really gaining steam.

Interestingly enough, as much as Ho Chi Minh would come to champion the cause of Vietnamese independence, he was thoroughly a Francophile. Many casual outside observers of history may not be aware of it, but Ho Chi Minh, in many ways, was immersed in the French language and culture. Sure, he still spoke his ancestral tongue and practiced ancestral customs, but there was also a side of Ho Chi Minh, just like among many of the French-educated Vietnamese elite, that was thoroughly French.

Ho Chi Minh loved the French language. When he briefly wrote for a French paper in the 1920s, he criticized other French journalists for supposedly "bastardizing" the French tongue by using expressions that mixed English and French. During a high-profile boxing match between French boxer Georges Carpentier and American boxer Ted Lewis, Ho Chi Minh lambasted the French press for mixing up English and French by inserting silly phrases such as "le manager" and "le challenger."[27]

Ho Chi Minh was the son of a Vietnamese civil servant in the employ of the French. He was not from a humble peasant background; he was actually part of the growing elite. Ho Chi Minh became an accomplished writer and wrote for many newspapers, periodicals, and other forms of mass media. He also served as a long-time editor of *Le Paria*, which was put out by a group of Africans and Asians in the Francophone world to discuss important matters to those in that community.

Ho Chi Minh in 1921.[17]

France, just like much of the rest of the world, suffered through the First World War. The war erupted in 1914 when a Serbian nationalist assassinated a visiting Austrian archduke in the Balkans, leading to tensions between Germany and Russia. France and England were yanked into the fight along with Russia.

---

[27] Karnow, Stanley. *Vietnam: A History*. Pg. 132.

At the onset of the war, many in the Vietnamese resistance movement saw an opportunity. France was distracted by the fighting in Europe. Vietnamese reformers thought that under such mounting stress abroad, France might be more amenable to Vietnamese demands. As France shifted its attention to the Western Front during World War I, revolutionary groups at home began to stir. Tensions grew even sharper when the colonial authorities started forcibly recruiting Vietnamese laborers and soldiers to aid the French war effort. Around 92,000 to 100,000 Vietnamese were sent to Europe, most as workers in munitions factories, shipyards, and other essential industries, with a smaller number serving in combat or support units.

For many of these men, the reasons behind the global conflict were utterly foreign. They had been plucked from their villages and shipped to the other side of the world to serve a cause they could barely comprehend and for a colonial power that often treated them with cold indifference.

Even so, time abroad proved eye-opening. Many returned to Vietnam with broader horizons and a better awareness of global politics. In a lesser-known episode, several hundred Vietnamese troops were dispatched toward the end of the war to join Allied forces in Siberia as part of the chaotic interventions following the Russian Revolution.

During the war, Russia was consumed by internal conflict, and a popular revolt turned into a communist-based revolution in 1917, which toppled the tsar. Shortly after, Russia was forced to sue for peace and sign an armistice with the Germans. This was a hollow victory for the Germans since the Western Front would collapse underneath them a short time later, and they would be forced to surrender and sign an armistice with Britain, France, and the United States.

Russia, in the meantime, was a cauldron of revolt and counter-revolt, and the Allies sent troops in to try to keep the peace. The Vietnamese battalion was placed in the middle of this. These Vietnamese "volunteers" were treated to a firsthand look at revolutionary communism on the Russian frontlines.

Ho Chi Minh left Vietnam in 1911 aboard a French steamer, working in the ship's galley. Over the next few years, he traveled widely, visiting ports in Africa, Europe, and eventually North America. By 1912 or 1913, he is believed to have set foot in the United States, probably working briefly in Boston and possibly in New York. Later accounts suggest he explored parts of the city and took in the sight of skyscrapers, a spectacle far removed from anything he had known in Vietnam.

His time in the United States was brief, but the ideas of liberty and self-determination that he encountered abroad would linger with him. Decades later, when he proclaimed Vietnam's independence in 1945, he deliberately echoed the words of America's own Declaration of Independence, an appeal that was both symbolic and strategic, though it was ultimately unsuccessful in gaining US support.

By 1914, Ho Chi Minh had made his way to London, where he found work in the kitchens of hotels, including the prestigious Carlton. Life in Britain offered new experiences and a window into the political movements of the time, including Irish resistance to British rule, which would have been hard to miss in the capital.

The arguments for Ireland's Home Rule were in full force during World War I. Despite the major war effort taking place in Europe, there were still plenty of Irish revolutionaries vocalizing the need for a free and independent Irish state. Ho Chi Minh absorbed these sentiments even as he internalized Vietnam's own problems. He thought about how Vietnam could try to shake the French yoke off its back just as the Irish were trying to shake off the British.

This front-row seat to Ireland's struggles proved to be an interesting lesson for Ho Chi Minh, but his visit to Paris would prove to be the most consequential. Here, he encountered several fellow Vietnamese expats whom he could easily persuade to join his cause for Vietnamese freedom.

He might not have been calling for a militant overthrow at this point, but Ho Chi Minh was at least raising the question and seeking out like-minded souls he could rely upon for future efforts. He found these souls in Paris. He also found Marxists—avid followers of Karl Marx's communist doctrine. These Parisian communists quickly turned the disillusioned Ho Chi Minh onto their dogma.

Ho Chi Minh remained in Paris throughout the closing stages of the First World War and was still there in 1919 when the Treaty of Versailles was being negotiated. He followed the events closely, paying particular attention to the arrival of US President Woodrow Wilson, whose talk of self-determination seemed—at least on the surface—to suggest a new era for subject peoples everywhere. Sensing a rare opportunity, Ho Chi Minh prepared a short petition addressed to the

Allied Powers, urging that Vietnam be granted greater political rights and reforms under French rule.

It was not a demand for immediate independence, but it did call for freedom of the press, the release of political prisoners, and a constitutional framework for Vietnamese governance. The petition never reached Wilson directly—it was handed to French officials, and no action was taken—but it marked Ho Chi Minh's first real foray into international politics.

While the Versailles conference came and went without change for Vietnam, Ho Chi Minh's activism brought him into contact with influential French socialists, such as Jean Longuet and Leon Blum. They invited him to the Congress of Tours in December 1920, where the French Socialist Party split. Ho Chi Minh—seeing the future in the more radical faction—chose to align himself with the newly formed French Communist Party.[28]

The meeting drew an array of socialist and communist thinkers eager to debate how best to put their ideals into practice. Into this lively forum stepped Ho Chi Minh, making his case for Vietnam's right to self-determination. Rather than laying out a detailed political program, he spoke in broad, urgent terms, calling on all factions of the left to unite behind Vietnam's struggle against what he saw as the oppressive grip of French colonialism.

Ho Chi Minh's approach at the Congress of Tours suggested that, at this stage, communism was less a matter of deep ideological commitment for him than a potential means to an end. This became a recurring theme in Vietnamese revolutionary politics. Ideology was to be used as a tool rather than an unshakable creed. Later, when the United States confronted communist North Vietnam, many in the West saw the conflict purely in ideological terms, missing the more pragmatic reality that for Ho Chi Minh and many of his compatriots, communism had begun as a strategic vehicle for liberation.

Historian Stanley Karnow later observed that Ho was initially comfortable among moderate socialists but came to see that the revolutionary communists, unlike the more cautious socialists, were willing to take decisive action against colonial rule. Communism also came with the promise of support from the Soviet Union, which would

---

[28] Karnow, Stanley. *Vietnam: A History.* Pg. 133.

be an invaluable ally. For Ho Chi Minh, aligning with the communists was above all a practical choice. And in 1920, it appeared to be the most effective route to ending French domination of Vietnam.[29]

---

[29] Karnow, Stanley. *Vietnam: A History.* Pg. 133.

Chapter 7: Vietnam Between the World Wars

"A country is not conquered and pacified by crushing its people through terror. After overcoming their initial fear, the masses grow increasingly rebellious, their accumulated bitterness steadily rising in reaction to the brutal use of force."

-French General Joseph Gallieni[30]

Just after the First World War came to a close, Ho Chi Minh became involved with the radicals of Paris. Paris back then—as is the case now—was a big city, and it was quite easy to get lost in the shuffle. Even so, Ho Chi Minh began to gain the attention of the French secret police, which began to monitor him in earnest in the 1920s.[31]

Just as his revolutionary work was expanding, Ho Chi Minh left France in 1923 or 1924 and headed to that bubbling cauldron of communist experimentation—the Soviet Union. Soviet Russia was an entrancing mecca for Ho. And as resourceful as ever, he found a means to support himself, enrolling at the Communist University of the Toilers of the East and working with the Comintern in Russia's capital of Moscow.

Ho Chi Minh did not just sit on the sidelines. He threw himself right into the mix and attended meetings and events where Soviet notables,

---

[30] Karnow, Stanley. *Vietnam: A History*. Pg. 119.
[31] Karnow, Stanley. *Vietnam: A History*. Pg. 134.

such as Joseph Stalin and Leon Trotsky, were present. It was an interim period of political tumult in Soviet Russia since Soviet leader Vladimir Lenin had just passed. In the aftermath of his death, Stalin and Trotsky were both potential successors. They became locked in a deadly struggle for supremacy.

Trotsky ultimately lost this contest and fled the Soviet Union. He would later be found dead in Mexico, the apparent victim of an assassination sponsored by Joseph Stalin. It was into this ideological fray that Ho Chi Minh had stepped. He learned a lot while he was in Moscow, especially as it pertained to party structure and political organizing. He would later take these skills back with him to Asia—and ultimately to Vietnam—where he laid out the framework for Vietnam's own eventual communist revolution.

But before returning to Vietnam, he would make a pitstop in Canton. China had not yet had its communist revolution, but its planning was already in the works. Ever since the fall of China's Qing dynasty in 1911, various factions had been struggling to gain prominence. The most prominent of these factions was the one that was being led by Chinese revolutionary Sun Yat-sen, which had called for the establishment of a Chinese republic.

Communist revolutionaries were also gaining footing and seeking to take advantage of the chaotic void the downfall of the Qing had left. They clamored for a communist Chinese state. Just a few years prior to Ho Chi Minh's arrival, the CCP (the Communist Party of China) was officially established, having come into being in 1921. Interestingly, even though the CCP was already in existence, Soviet Russia's official contacts in China were through the Chinese Nationalists, who favored Sun Yat-sen's notion of a Chinese republic.

At this time, the Nationalists were being led by Sun Yat-sen's successor, Chiang Kai-shek. An official Soviet liaison had been established between Chiang Kai-shek and a Soviet official named Mikhail Borodin. The Soviets did this out of pragmatism. They wanted to have relations with China, and they saw the Nationalists as the strongest faction and the most reliable partner in the region.

Ho Chi Minh became acquainted with Borodin and was actually enlisted to be his personal interpreter. Minh was quite skilled with language, after all, as he was fluent in French, Vietnamese, and many Chinese dialects. Ho Chi Minh was also a voracious writer and penned several opinion pieces for communist papers.[32] And when he was not writing about what others should do, Ho was actively doing it. Ho Chi Minh became quite busy as an organizer, managing to cobble together a group of radical Vietnamese communists in southern China, with whom he formed the Thanh Nien Cach Mang Dong Chi Hoi or, as it would be rendered in English, "The Revolutionary Youth League."[33]

It is important to note that the Chinese Nationalists and the Chinese Communists had a sort of mutual understanding with each other at this time. Although the Chinese Nationalists were in the ascendancy, they did not much bother with the Communists as long as they did not get in their way. It was only when the Communists began to gain support that the Chinese Nationalists became alarmed and began to push back against them.

In 1927, the Nationalists finally decided they had reached the end of their tolerance and began actively hunting the Communists. Many were killed when violence broke out in Chinese cities between the two factions, and Ho Chi Minh was forced to flee. He left for Moscow before heading to western Europe.

Ho Chi Minh seems as if he were a bit adrift during this period, moving between Moscow, Paris, and other European cities while carrying out assignments for the Comintern. He was likely in a state of shock and disillusionment over the eruption of internecine violence in China and was simply taking some time to regroup as he quietly plotted his next move.

He stopped for a short spell in Paris as he further contemplated his state of affairs before departing the European continent. The following year, Ho Chi Minh was all the way over in Bangkok, which was then the seat of governance of Siam (modern-day Thailand). Here, he lived among the Vietnamese exile community and spent time around Buddhist temples, adopting a low-profile appearance to blend in with the locals. However, rather than preaching the tenets of Buddhism, Ho Chi Minh was preaching the tenets of revolution and communism.

Back in Vietnam, revolutionary movements were gaining momentum. One group, in particular, the Viet Nam Quoc Dan Dang, or "VNQDD" for short, became powerful enough to gain the attention of the French

---

[32] Karnow, Stanley. *Vietnam: A History.* Pgs. 134-135.
[33] Karnow, Stanley. *Vietnam: A History.* Pg. 135.

army. The French air force even went as far as to engage in wholesale bombing of villages believed to be hiding networks of the VNQDD.

The VNQDD was not a communist group; it actually got its start with the help of some of Chiang Kai-shek's own Nationalists, who were actively battling the Communists in China. The fact that the French were ready to wage war against Communists or Nationalists shows that the French could have really cared less about the ideology of Vietnamese freedom fighters. The main priority of the French was to squash any talk of freedom and independence from French rule as quickly as possible. This was in stark contrast to the United States, which primarily waged a war in Vietnam to prevent the spread of communism in the region. It makes one wonder what could have happened if the French had allowed a non-communist strain of Vietnamese independence to blossom. Perhaps if the French had allowed a nationalistic and staunchly anti-communist regime to flourish in Vietnam, such a regime might have become an ally and partner of the US during the Cold War.

Nevertheless, at this stage in the game, the French imperialists were indiscriminately tamping down any factions seeking independence. Whether they were socialist, communist, or nationalist meant very little to French colonial administrators at the time. And as the struggle between the French colonial regime and the VNQDD persisted, it became very ugly. In 1929, the VNQDD staged the assassination of a prominent French official, Alfred Bazin. Bazin was an integral part of the colony's functionality since he oversaw the recruitment of large numbers of Vietnamese workers—often under coercion, low pay, brutal conditions, and distant postings. So, it was not much of a surprise that he was targeted.[34]

Bazin was leaving the home of his mistress in Hanoi when the assassin got the drop on him. The very next day, on February 10th, 1930, VNQDD members launched the Yen Bay Mutiny, in which Vietnamese soldiers in the French colonial army rebelled, attacking their French officers. The VNQDD hoped this would spark a general insurrection across northern Vietnam.

As much as the VNQDD might have been patting themselves on their backs for succeeding in such a brazen hit, their joy would not last for long. The mutiny was crushed within days, and then the French dropped the hammer.

---

[34] Karnow, Stanley. *Vietnam: A History.* Pg. 135.

A massive crackdown was unleashed, which saw the VNQDD ruthlessly hunted down. A huge number of them were arrested.[35] Many others were killed; some of them were executed right on the spot. According to writer and historian Stanley Karnow, the French even went as far as to roll out the guillotine to chop off the heads of VNQDD leaders.[36] It is not clear if this was a matter of convenience or some kind of symbolism. The guillotine had become synonymous with excess retribution ever since the days of the French Revolution, when it was dropping left and right upon the heads of ideologues and partisans of all stripes.

That same year, the stock market in the United States. Initially, perhaps it did not seem to mean too much to the French, but the stock market crash in the United States would have global repercussions. The 1929 stock market crash would ultimately lead to a global economic crisis, which has often been referred to as the Great Depression.

One of the reasons the economic downturn in the US affected other parts of the world was America's sudden decrease in imports, which, of course, severely affected export-heavy nations like Vietnam. The French had transformed Vietnam into an export economy. Vietnam regularly exported valuable goods such as coal, rubber, lumber, and rice. However, in the aftermath of the crash and the subsequent economic depression, no one was buying the goods that Vietnam was selling. This meant that colonial coffers started to go dry, leading to shortages of staples that the average Vietnamese had come to depend on. The sudden scarcity affected already struggling Vietnamese communities.

Ho Chi Minh went to Hong Kong in 1929. At the time, Hong Kong was a British colony. There, he began to put together a group of several communist factions, which were dubbed the Indochinese Communist Party. This group championed the revolutionary overthrow of the French from all of French Indochina. Ho Chi Minh and his cohorts were able to gain recognition for their cause and began organizing strikes and labor protests back in Vietnam.

However, the Hong Kong police, under pressure from French authorities who wanted him arrested and extradited, were soon on the trail of Ho Chi Minh, and he was arrested in 1931. Ho still had some

---

[35] Karnow, Stanley. *Vietnam: A History*. Pg. 136.
[36] Karnow, Stanley. *Vietnam: A History*. Pg. 136.

cards left to play. He threw himself on the sympathy of the British colonial administration of Hong Kong, citing his poor health. He ended up in a hospital before he managed to leave Hong Kong and make his way to China.

His departure was so abrupt that reports of his death began to circulate. His obituary even surfaced in the Soviet press. The French, who had also been pursuing him, apparently closed his police file around this time, reportedly noting that Ho Chi Minh had died in Hong Kong. Whether French intelligence truly believed he was dead or simply lost track of him remains unclear, but Ho Chi Minh effectively disappeared from public view for several years, allowing him to continue his work underground.[37]

This sounds like the stuff of a thriller novel, but this was indeed Ho Chi Minh's real-life story. Ho continued his globe-trotting as the rest of the world around him continued to unravel.

During the 1930s, economies all over the world, one after the other, began to go into decline. Those that were the hardest hit were either the countries that were most often on the back foot and oppressed, like Vietnam, or those that had come out on the losing side of World War I, like Germany. This economic unrest and general instability, both in Vietnam and in many other parts of the world, ultimately set the stage for the Second World War.

---

[37] Karnow, Stanley. *Vietnam: A History.* Pg. 136.

Chapter 8: The Japanese Occupation During World War II

"Peasants came in from the nearby provinces on foot, leaning on each other, carrying their children in baskets. They dug in garbage piles, looking for anything at all. Banana skins, orange peels, discarded greens. They even ate rats. But they couldn't get enough to keep alive. They tried to beg, but everyone else was hungry, and they would drop dead in the streets. Every morning, when I opened my door, I found five or six corpses on the step."

-Tran Duy Hung[38]

The early 1930s marked a period of great change, not just for Vietnam but also for the whole world. In Vietnam, the system the French used to govern their colonial subjects was rapidly breaking down. They had installed their own puppet ruler in the form of the supposed emperor, Bao Dai, but he was nothing more than a figurehead. Bao Dai was generally despised by the populace. In some ways, Bao Dai was despised even more than the French since it seemed as if Bao Dai, a young ruler, spent most of his life in lavish luxury while his people suffered. This only served to remind the Vietnamese of their dilemma.

Ho Chi Minh continued to travel, keeping abreast of all the latest developments. In 1940, Southeast Asia was suddenly shaken up by

---

[38] Karnow, Stanley. *Vietnam: A History.* Pg. 160.

ramped-up aggression from Japan.³⁹ Japan had aligned itself with Nazi Germany, which had risen up from the ashes after Germany's defeat in World War I. While the Germans were busy saber-rattling in Europe throughout the 1930s, Japan was bullying many of its neighbors in East Asia. The Japanese launched a brutal invasion of China, which included the infamous Rape of Nanking.

By 1940, Japan had begun to swoop down on Southeast Asia, coming much closer to the shores of Vietnam. The incident that triggered this aggression was when their allied partner, Germany, managed to topple France in 1940, forcing the French to sign an armistice agreement. The Germans were able to then seize and occupy a huge chunk of northern France, leaving just a French rump state centered around the southern French town of Vichy.

According to the terms of the agreement, the new Vichy France government was allowed to keep what remained of its colonial empire in North Africa, Southeast Asia, and elsewhere. Even so, the Japanese acted, sensing the weakness of the French. Although the French were ostensibly "on good terms" with the Nazis, the Japanese showed they had their own ideas and began making their own demands on the French.

The world was indeed a complicated place in 1940. World War II had just begun, but the opposing sides had not entirely formed. For instance, the United States was not yet in the war. The Soviet Union had signed a non-aggression pact with Nazi Germany and had even participated in the joint invasion of Poland in 1939, which is widely recognized as the start of World War II.

Joseph Stalin's pact encouraged communists all over the world not to make any aggressive moves toward the Axis Powers of Germany, Japan, and Italy. But that certainly put the Communists of China in a strange position since they were being slaughtered by Japanese troops. Even stranger was the fact that Germany had actually rendered limited aid to China before cutting it off in favor of shoring up stronger relations with Japan.

In 1940, the lines of battle were quite murky. It was not until Adolf Hitler decided to double-cross Stalin and invade Russia in June 1941 and Japan decided to bomb Pearl Harbor in Hawaii in December 1941

---

³⁹ Karnow, Stanley. *Vietnam: A History.* Pg. 137.

that everything changed. After this point, the lines had been firmly drawn, and everyone knew what side they were on. Well, almost everyone.

In Vietnam, like in many other parts of East Asia, it was more complex. Initially, many former colonial subjects welcomed the Japanese as liberators. After all, they had seen the Japanese knock out hated colonial administrations. However, it did not take long for these supposed liberators to be perceived as ruthless and brutal.

Ho Chi Minh never even considered siding with the Japanese. For him, the wisest, most pragmatic wartime strategy was to align with the Allies, aid them in defeating the Japanese, and then request full liberation from France at the end of the war. Just as he had done after World War I with US President Woodrow Wilson, Ho Chi Minh pinned his hopes on the United States. He thought the US would restrain the French and allow the Vietnamese to finally embark upon a course of their own self-determination.

His views would prove to be short-sighted. Not only did he underestimate the potential for goodwill on the part of American victors, but he also did not foresee the coming Cold War that would make the West view communism as being akin to the plague. Prior to World War II and even during the war, communism was kept at arm's length, but it was not yet perceived as a dire threat to civilization. This all changed after the war when Western democracies, led by the United States, and the communist bloc, led by the Soviet Union, began to stare each other down in hotspots such as West and East Germany and North and South Korea. Little did Ho Chi Minh know that North and South Vietnam would become one of these geopolitical hotspots and one that the United States would come to view as of the utmost importance.

By 1940, Japan had muscled its way into French Indochina. But instead of booting out the colonial authorities, the Japanese simply let the French administrators stay; they were just under Japanese oversight. It was an arrangement of convenience. The Japanese got the access and resources they wanted, and the French, battered by their defeat in Europe and taking orders from Vichy France, mostly played along.

Sure, there might have been some murmurs of resistance behind the scenes, but for the most part, the French rolled over. They maintained their posts, kept the colonial machinery humming, and served the Japanese agenda. This uneasy alliance didn't fool many Vietnamese.

After all, what kind of liberation keeps the same old colonial masters in power? Japan talked a big game about freeing Asia from Western imperialism, but in Indochina, all they really did was put a new face on the same old system.

The Japanese were even worse exploiters than the French, seizing all of the raw materials they could to help keep their war machine running. They also tried to turn northern Vietnam into a staging ground for further attacks on China to the north, stationing tens of thousands of troops in the region.

Ho Chi Minh returned to northern Vietnam in 1941, where he established the Viet Minh Front to wage guerrilla war against both the Japanese occupiers and their French collaborators. During the war, the US Army's OSS (the precursor to the CIA) came into contact with Ho and his forces. They struck a deal. The OSS would supply training, weapons, and medicine, while Ho Chi Minh would provide intelligence and guerrilla support against the Japanese. For a brief moment, the man who would later become Washington's nemesis was working hand in hand with American operatives.

Along with providing intelligence, Ho Chi Minh proved to be a gifted recruiter, convincing ordinary villagers to join his cause. He avoided bogging people down with Marxist theory, instead speaking in simple terms of life, liberty, and survival. During the catastrophic famine of 1945, when between one and two million Vietnamese starved to death, the Viet Minh stepped in where the French and Japanese had failed. They seized rice from warehouses and granaries to redistribute it to hungry peasants. This was not just relief—it was also political theater, proof that the Viet Minh could protect and

Ho Chi Minh in 1946.[18]

provide in ways the old rulers could not. For many, the fact that food reached their villages during those desperate months was reason enough to pledge allegiance to Ho Chi Minh's movement.

As the war continued to progress, the Japanese finally ripped away the illusion of continued French governance, removing colonial administrators from power in French Indochina in the spring of 1945. In their place, they set up the Empire of Vietnam, with the former puppet of the French—Bao Dai—as its so-called emperor.

Just prior to the war's end, the Japanese had developed a strategy of making a last stand in Southeast Asia. They knew they were losing ground and that the Allies were boxing them in, so they wanted to create several fortified positions near Japan in order to stall and stymie the Allied forces as much as possible. They intended for Vietnam to be one of these fortified fallback positions.

However, after the United States shocked the world by dropping atomic bombs on Japan, the Japanese scrapped this plan. The cities of Hiroshima and Nagasaki were utterly destroyed by atomic weapons, and the Americans let the Japanese know in no uncertain terms that they had more where that came from. This threat of nuclear annihilation finally made Japan surrender and come to the table. The war was over. There would be no need for a dramatic last stand for Japan in Southeast Asia after all. However, Vietnam's own last stand for freedom from outside control was not yet over. Not by a long shot.

Chapter 9: The August Revolution and the First Indochina War

"You would understand better if you could see what is happening here, if you could feel this yearning for independence that is in everyone's heart, and which no human force can any longer restrain. Should you reestablish a French administration here, it will not be obeyed. Every village will be a nest of resistance, each former collaborator an enemy, and your officials and colonists will themselves seek to leave this atmosphere, which will choke them."

-*Bao Dai*[40]

As Japan crumbled during the last days of World War II, Ho Chi Minh's forces, which were underground and organizing in northern Vietnam, were actively positioning themselves throughout the region. When Japan announced its surrender on August 15th, 1945, the Japanese were too weakened and unwilling to defend the Bao Dai puppet administration they had installed.

Ho Chi Minh saw his opportunity. In what became known as the August Revolution, Viet Minh forces moved swiftly to exploit the collapse of Japanese and French control. Between mid-August and the end of August, when Emperor Bao Dai formally abdicated, they organized mass demonstrations and seized government buildings across the country. Minh and his troops essentially stepped into a vacuum, moving in just as Japanese authority collapsed.

---

[40] Karnow, Stanley. *Vietnam: A History.* Pg. 163.

As much as revolutions are lionized, they are often quite ugly. In any situation in which one section of society seeks to topple another, it usually involves violence of the most grotesque kind. During the French Revolution, for example, poor, starving peasants believed that the rich were causing all of their problems and stormed into the Bastille, ready to rip French soldiers apart with their bare hands.

Similar, ugly scenes like this were repeated in Vietnam. Ho Chi Minh not only enabled his Viet Minh forces to storm into government compounds, but he also unleashed a mob of peasants. These starving Vietnamese peasants stormed into the homes of the rich and powerful. Those who had prospered under the colonial regime were ruthlessly targeted. Anyone who had profited from the French colonial government or collaborated with the hated Japanese occupiers was deemed a traitor of Vietnam.

Sure, some colonial administrators might have been exploitive and abusive, and some of those who collaborated with the Japanese likely deserved some form of punishment. However, angry mobs are not the best choice when it comes to dishing out fair and unbiased justice. As such, the situation in Vietnam became very ugly, very fast.

Emperor Bao Dai could see which way the wind was blowing. With Japan defeated and the Viet Minh revolution rolling through the country, he knew his days on the throne were numbered. Rather than wait for the crowds to storm his gates, he chose to bow out on his own terms. He declared that he would rather be a citizen of an independent nation than an emperor of a broken one. Handing over the imperial seal and sword, he quietly closed the chapter on Vietnam's centuries of monarchy.[41] The Viet Minh, recognizing the value of his imperial name, kept him on as a kind of "supreme adviser" to lend a touch of legitimacy to their cause.

On September 2nd, 1945, Ho Chi Minh officially announced the creation of the Democratic Republic of Vietnam, or the "DRV" for short. This was the same day the Japanese had formally surrendered to the Allies. Japanese garrisons still occupied the country, though they had officially laid down arms. The postwar chaos was so great that the Allies, lacking immediate manpower of their own, leaned on these defeated Japanese troops to enforce order and impose martial law until British and Chinese forces could move in. As bizarre bedfellows as they might have been, the British, French, and even the defeated Japanese worked

---

[41] Karnow, Stanley. *Vietnam: A History.* Pg. 162.

side by side in the south to patrol Vietnam and restore a semblance of order. This coalition of convenience pushed the Viet Minh out of Saigon and paved the way for the French colonial administration to return, at least in Cochinchina. North Vietnam, meanwhile, was still beyond their grasp, under the uneasy watch of Chinese Nationalist troops and Ho Chi Minh's Viet Minh.

The fact that Vietnam would be divided between the North and the South seemed to be a given. Not only was there a long, historic precedent for this division (going all the way back to the Kingdom of Champa), but it so happens that the heads of the Allied Powers had met in Potsdam in July of 1945, right before Japan surrendered, to discuss this issue. It was determined that Vietnam should be split in half at the 16th parallel (later at the 17th parallel) so that the British (and ostensibly the French) could take control of the South, while the Chinese would man the North. This pattern of sharing the burden of occupying postwar nations was a common theme after World War II.

The main instigator of the war, Germany, had been split up into sections, with the Soviet Union agreeing to occupy a large chunk of East Germany, while the British, Americans, and French occupied the western portion (later unifying their western shares into one West Germany). Korea had also been split in half, creating a communist North Korea (which, as of this writing, still exists) and a democratic South Korea. Japan likely would have been similarly divided if the Americans had not so thoroughly forced it into submission. The US took control of Japan without the need for a Russian invasion and occupation.

At any rate, Vietnam's fate was decided along very similar lines of demarcation. As mentioned, the Chinese Nationalists under Chiang Kai-shek were tasked with overseeing northern Vietnam. It is important to note the immediate state of postwar China in late 1945. The Chinese Nationalists had temporarily teamed up with their rivals, the Communists, to defeat the Japanese. Now that the war was over, the slow-burning civil war had erupted, and it would soon ramp up. By 1949, the Communists would shock the world by defeating the Nationalists and driving them off the mainland. The Nationalists ended up seeking refuge in Taiwan, which had just been seized from Japan, and founded a separate Chinese government there. As of this writing, the government founded by the Nationalists still exists and still insists on being separate from China, even though China constantly clamors about reclaiming it.

Back in 1945, though, the Nationalists were still in the ascendancy and were the main power in China. When asked by the Western allies to help with the situation in Vietnam, the Chinese sent in troops to watch over northern Vietnam.

However, most of these troops were ill-equipped, and many were starving and dressed in rags. Rather than safeguarding the north, the Chinese troops are said to have acted more like bandits, periodically raiding local businesses and even homes for food and other supplies. There were times they even raided farms and stole livestock. Needless to say, it did not take long for these supposed keepers of the peace to overstay their welcome.

Even so, Ho Chi Minh wanted to appease the Chinese as much as possible so that they could help him consolidate his own power. The Chinese in the north were under the command of Chinese General Lu Han, and Ho Chi Minh was sure to cozy up to Lu Han, overlooking even the worst of his trespasses.

With the Chinese breathing down their necks in the north, Ho Chi Minh was prepared to signal some kind of agreement with the French. At one point, he even spoke at length about how he had admiration for the French and French culture and about how he had no desire to completely sever the historic and cultural link they had with the French nation. There is likely some truth in this. Many aspects of French culture had indeed become ingrained with the Vietnamese by this point, and Ho was a bit of a Francophile himself.

But even so, this was certainly an extreme amount of whitewashing on Ho's part. Because no matter how much some Vietnamese might have admired certain aspects of French culture, that admiration did not erase the animosity that had built up during colonialism. One might have been a fan of Victor Hugo and enjoy an occasional crepe or croissant, but that does not mean they also enjoyed being lorded over by French colonial administrators.

Nevertheless, Ho Chi Minh was ready to begin talks. He had a high-profile meeting with General Philippe Leclerc, the French commander sent to reestablish France's hold on Indochina. Ho's most immediate demand was clear—he wanted Vietnam to remain whole and united. The French insisted on preserving their authority.

After a long and strenuous round of discussions, the two sides came to an agreement on March 6th, 1946. France would recognize the

Democratic Republic of Vietnam as a "free state" within the French Union, while French troops would be allowed back into the north to replace the departing Chinese forces. It was a fragile compromise at best, and even as the ink was drying, skirmishes flared between the two sides, especially in the South.[42]

In late 1946, talks would break down completely. Tensions had been building throughout the year as the French attempted to reassert colonial control while Ho Chi Minh demanded full independence. The final breaking point came in November 1946 when French forces bombarded the port city of Haiphong, killing thousands of Vietnamese civilians in a dispute over customs control. On December 19th, Viet Minh forces attacked French positions in Hanoi, and the French embarked upon a major military offensive in response. This was the start of the First Indochina War, a brutal eight-year conflict that would claim hundreds of thousands of lives. French forces employed aerial bombardment, napalm, and the destruction of villages in their efforts to crush the Viet Minh, while guerrilla warfare tactics led to violence against civilians on both sides.

The French felt that they had lost quite a bit of legitimacy, so they reinstalled the toppled Vietnamese emperor, Bao Dai, this time in the South. At first, they experimented with an "Autonomous Republic of Cochinchina," but it was little more than a colonial façade. However, by mid-1949, the French went further. On July 1st, they declared the creation of the State of Vietnam, with Bao Dai as its head of state. Though billed as independent, the new state remained firmly bound within the French Union. It was essentially a rebranded version of France's colonial empire. France still held sway over the army, diplomacy, and much of the economy.

By this time, the Cold War was in full swing. The Soviet Union was threatening Europe, and China had become a full-blown communist nation. The United States had come out firmly on the side of South Vietnam in a bid to stave off what they feared was just the start of a massive wave of communism that threatened to engulf all of Southeast Asia.

American war planners were quite alarmed to learn of the complete defeat of French forces by the Viet Minh in May 1954 at the Battle of

---

[42] Karnow, Stanley. *Vietnam: A History*. Pg. 169.

Dien Bien Phu. Up until this point, the Viet Minh forces had primarily relied on hit-and-run, ambush-style attacks. But it was here, out in the open, in a valley region known as Dien Bien Phu, that the Viet Minh decided to roll the dice and take a decisive stand.

Giving it everything they had, the Vietnamese initially launched aggressive infantry assaults against entrenched French positions—attacks that at times seemed almost suicidal. These charges were shocking to behold, but after sustaining a high number of casualties, the Vietnamese adjusted their tactics. They shifted gears, hauling heavy artillery into the hills that surrounded the valley. They used that high ground to unleash withering fire on the French positions below. Suddenly, the tables were turned, and it was the French who found themselves out in the open, being decimated by the Vietnamese.

Ultimately, this defeat dragged France back to the negotiating table, but this time around, North Vietnam was playing for keeps. In a deal brokered at Geneva by multiple world powers, including the United Kingdom, the Soviet Union, and China, Vietnam was divided not along the 16th parallel, but farther south, along the 17th parallel. Ho Chi Minh's communist DRV would take the north, while a non-communist, Western-backed government would be set up in the south.

The French were forced to wash their hands of their little project in South Vietnam, and the South Vietnamese would, for a time, have to fend for themselves. That is, of course, until the United States became involved.

Chapter 10: The Vietnam War: A Nation Divided

"Though our soldiers have fought gloriously, we are still far from victory. Though our administration is honest and efficient, corruption has not been eliminated. Though we have introduced reforms, disorder disturbs several areas. We could ascribe these setbacks to the fact that our regime is young, or make other excuses. But no. Our successes are due to the efforts of our citizens, and our shortcomings are our own fault."

-Ho Chi Minh[43]

Although the United States would not have a large troop presence on the ground in Vietnam until the mid-1960s, the Americans were involved just about as soon as the French left. The French left Vietnam divided, with a communist North and a Western-backed regime in the South. America carried the torch from the French, and by the late 1950s, it was actively involved with the fledgling capitalist democracy in South Vietnam, sending money, arms, and advisers on a regular basis in the hopes of bolstering its defenses against the ever-encroaching North Vietnamese.

Making matters even more worrisome for the United States, North Vietnam had gained the full backing of the communist bloc. In 1950, both the Soviet Union and China voiced their support for the North Vietnamese, recognizing the communist state. This made the US more

---

[43] Karnow, Stanley. *Vietnam: A History.* Pg. 168.

determined than ever to support the South Vietnamese military, which at that time was called the Vietnamese National Army.

Bao Dai was like a royal ping pong ball. He kept getting batted about from one group to another. Since he was a direct descendant of the great Vietnamese Emperor Gia Long, his credentials were not in doubt. Prior to the outbreak of World War II, he had been the puppet of the French. He sat on a throne and pretended to be in charge while the French called the shots. After Japan invaded and occupied French Indochina, he became the plaything of the Japanese. They used him to present some sort of legitimacy to their presence/intervention in Vietnamese affairs.

After the war, Bao Dai resigned from his post and, for a time, resided in North Vietnam, where he served as an "adviser" to Ho Chi Minh. As mentioned earlier, the pragmatic Bao Dai managed to go with the flow and rode the oncoming current of communism. With Bao Dai in their midst, it was as if the North Vietnamese had suddenly been given the royal seal of approval. Ho Chi Minh hoped to use Bao Dai to give himself and his regime an air of legitimacy, appointing the former emperor as "supreme advisor."

However, Bao Dai quickly realized he held no real power in the communist government and was being used merely as a symbolic figurehead. Uncomfortable with communist ideology and feeling sidelined, he grew disillusioned with the arrangement. In March 1946, he was sent on a diplomatic mission to China and decided not to return. He fled to Hong Kong, where he would remain until the French brought him back in 1949 to serve as emperor of their rival puppet government.

On March 8th, 1949, Bao Dai and the French signed what became known as the Élysée Agreement. This marked the beginning of France's so-called "Bao Dai Solution," with Bao Dai nominally restored as chief of state of Vietnam. On paper, he was in charge of domestic affairs, while the French still clung to military and diplomatic power. In practice, Bao Dai's authority extended little beyond the French-controlled south. Even so, the arrangement gained international traction. In early 1950, the United States moved to recognize Bao Dai's government, just as the Soviets and Chinese officially recognized Ho Chi Minh's rival regime in Hanoi.[44]

---

[44] Karnow, Stanley. *Vietnam: A History*. Pg. 190.

This seemingly made sure that the Cold War stage was set. The US even went as far as to set up an embassy in Saigon to further establish a sense of legitimacy. However, the early 1950s often had the French both accepting American aid and resenting American interference. The French were more than willing to take American money and arms, but they resisted the notion of American military advisers, whom they saw as being too intrusive.[45]

Any real cooperation between the French and the Americans fell through when the French army was thoroughly defeated by North Vietnam in 1954. Even so, Bao Dai remained in place. It was then the Americans' turn to use Bao Dai as their own pawn in the larger geopolitical strategies of the Cold War.

The Americans feared the spread of communism and wished to contain it at all costs. Countless lives would be lost in the effort to keep the communist North from crossing that arbitrarily drawn line of the 17th parallel and heading south. Making matters even more difficult for

North and South Vietnam.[19]

the Americans was the fact that both the French and Bao Dai had thoroughly corrupted the government of South Vietnam. The notion that the regime of South Vietnam could somehow win the hearts and minds of the Vietnamese masses was pretty ludicrous.

---

[45] Karnow, Stanley. *Vietnam: A History.* Pg. 195.

The increasingly cynical Bao Dai had learned to rely on Vietnam's underworld bosses to supplement his income. His own generals often dipped into underworld pots such as casinos, opium dens, and houses of ill repute.[46] Bao Dai used these corrupt institutions to glean extra money for himself, and he also had come to use underworld thugs as his own personal enforcers.

The French also began recruiting from the same sources. By doing this, the French and Bao Dai managed to bake a strong thread of corruption into the South Vietnamese cake. This thread of corruption would come to haunt the Americans as they tried their best to establish a respectable, capitalist democracy in South Vietnam that the common Vietnamese masses could rally behind.

It was hard to bolster national pride in a regime that the average Vietnamese villager viewed as a bunch of lecherous cronies and crooks. Even worse, corruption was fostered with the rise of the South Vietnamese prime minister, Ngo Dinh Diem. Bao Dai had made Ngo Dinh Diem his prime minister in 1954, and he then went on to be elected as the president of South Vietnam in 1955.

But why was Ngo Dinh Diem disliked? In order to understand the level of disdain that the Vietnamese had for him, one has to try to put themselves into the mindset of the average Vietnamese person at the time.

Vietnam had been under French colonial rule for over a century, followed by a brutal occupation by Japan. With Japan's defeat, the previously evicted French colonial overlords tried to reassert their authority. When direct rule didn't work, they used corrupt local puppets: Bao Dai and Ngo Dinh Diem. Many Vietnamese viewed both of them as a special blend of corrupt cronies and crooks, who were ultimately subservient to the interests of the French.

This situation helped the North Vietnamese convert many in the South, especially those in the rural countryside regions. These rural South Vietnamese supporters would become known as the Viet Cong. Officially established in 1960, the Viet Cong would come to play a crucial role in turning the tide of the war against the US and its allies.

As the Viet Cong gained strength, the corrupt and unpopular president of South Vietnam, Ngo Dinh Diem, tried to stamp out their

---

[46] Karnow, Stanley. *Vietnam: A History*. Pg. 196.

resistance. He did so in about the most brutal fashion possible. As unpopular as he might have already been, this forceful purge of communists in the South would only make him more of a political pariah than he already was. On the eve of the Viet Cong's official founding, in 1959, Ngo Dinh Diem issued his infamous Law 10/59. This law basically gave him unlimited authority to lock up and even execute anyone who was suspected of being complicit with the communists.

However, it was not long before the corrupt Diem government used the same law to persecute just about anyone who might be critical of his regime. Even worse, people began to turn on each other, and accusations began to fly left and right among those who did not like each other. Have a problem with your neighbor? Well, accuse them of being a communist! It was highly unethical, yet in such a troubling backdrop, these things became prevalent. It was truly a dreadful state of affairs, and it ultimately encouraged everyday Vietnamese to look toward the communist North as a solution to their many problems.

Near the end of 1963, the South Vietnamese regime of Ngo Dinh Diem collapsed. On November 1st, a group of Vietnamese generals launched a coup, backed indirectly by the United States, overthrowing Diem's rule. Overnight, Diem and his brother Nhu were arrested, and on November 2nd, they were assassinated. The US, having grown frustrated with Diem's autocratic style and his failure to win support against the communist insurgency, had signaled that it would not intervene to stop the coup.

This was pretty shocking, considering the fact that Diem visited the United States just a few years prior, in 1957. At the time, President Dwight D. Eisenhower hailed him as Vietnam's savior or, as he put it, "miracle man."[47] However, it seems that by 1963, the time for miracles had long since passed.

As an interesting aside, many have since openly speculated how strange it is that shortly after Diem's assassination, US President John F. Kennedy was also assassinated. Diem was killed on November 2nd, 1963, and John F. Kennedy was gunned down on November 22nd, 1963. It is fairly well known that the CIA colluded with elements of South Vietnam to take down Diem. Any talk of the CIA's involvement in John F. Kennedy's death remains purely in the realm of conspiracy theory,

---

[47] Karnow, Stanley. *Vietnam: A History.* Pg. 245.

though. In any case, it is said that upon hearing of Diem's passing, and just prior to his own, J.F.K. expressed deep sadness and concern for what was happening in Vietnam.

After Diem's ouster, the situation in South Vietnam only got worse. Ngo Dinh Diem was succeeded by Duong Van Minh, a hardline Vietnamese general of the South Vietnamese army, which was called the "ARVN," or Army of the Republic of Vietnam. Americans had placed their bets on him to be the tough guy who would clean house and get South Vietnam in order. It was hoped that he could bolster the armed forces and provide a more robust defense against the North while shoring up the strength of the South Vietnamese government. However, Duong Van Minh proved to be just as flawed as Diem, and the situation began to deteriorate. This led to a rather volatile situation in late 1963, which continued on into 1964. Immediate action had to be taken.

It fell to Lyndon B. Johnson to come to grips with the unraveling situation in Vietnam. The South Vietnamese government was faltering, unable to withstand the North's growing insurgency, and the United States concluded that more direct involvement was necessary. The pretext for this emerged on August 2nd, 1964, when the USS *Maddox* reported an encounter with North Vietnamese torpedo boats in the Gulf of Tonkin. Johnson ordered retaliatory air strikes a few days later.

On August 7th, 1964, Congress passed the Gulf of Tonkin Resolution, granting President Johnson sweeping authority to use military force in Vietnam. With the authorization secured, Johnson escalated the war, targeting North Vietnam's supply routes and infrastructure with an intense bombing campaign known as Operation Rolling Thunder, which was launched in March 1965.

Johnson hoped that heavy aerial bombardment and pressure on Hanoi's logistics would force them to back down or negotiate. Instead, the North dug in and fortified its defenses—and the United States found itself drawn ever deeper into the quagmire of Vietnam.

On the heels of this bombing blitz, the first American troops were placed in combat roles in Vietnam. By the end of 1965, there would be around 184,000 US troops in the region. This number would quickly balloon to well over 385,000 by the following year. Additionally, by 1967, hundreds of thousands of tons of explosives had been unleashed over North Vietnam, with the eventual total for the Rolling Thunder campaign reaching more than 640,000 tons.

US Navy A-6A Intruder all-weather bombers in 1968.[30]

In late 1967, the US still clung to the hope that sheer force of numbers could tip the balance. By that time, nearly half a million American troops were stationed in Vietnam, alongside an air campaign that continued to rain destruction on the North. If there was any single theme that military planners kept repeating, it was this elusive promise of "turning the tide." Just as the French commanders had parroted back to their political backers in France, US military commanders continually told political backers in Washington, DC, that they were just about to turn the corner. Just give them a little more time, money, troops, bombs, or what have you, and this war would be won.

This old song and dance was wearing very thin by the late 1960s. Troops and money kept pouring into Vietnam, and people were wondering where it would all lead. They kept being told that the war was almost over—that it was almost won—but no one was seeing any meaningful results. For the most part, the general public could only wonder and speculate as to what was really going on behind the scenes. That is, until they were granted a front-row seat due to reporting on the ground.

The shocking Tet Offensive erupted on January 30th, 1968. It was North Vietnam's surprise bid to ring in the Lunar New Year with a storm of fire. Over eighty thousand North Vietnamese and Viet Cong fighters hurled themselves into more than a hundred cities, towns, and military bases across South Vietnam. This was no minor raid. They hit provincial capitals, stormed airfields, and even blasted a hole into the walls of the US Embassy in Saigon.

The attacks were often suicidal, and US and South Vietnamese forces killed tens of thousands of enemy soldiers in the process. However, the damage had been done. It was clear that the communists could strike anywhere, at any time. One of the bloodiest battles unfolded in Hue, where communist forces seized control of much of the city. For weeks, US Marines and South Vietnamese troops clawed their way through the streets, house by house, until Hue was retaken. When the smoke cleared, mass graves were found—evidence that communists had executed thousands of officials, clergy, and civilians during their brief rule.

Militarily, Tet was a disaster for North Vietnam. They lost perhaps forty thousand to fifty thousand fighters. But politically and psychologically, the Tet Offensive was a triumph. The images of chaos on American television screens told a different story from battlefield statistics. For years, US leaders had promised that victory was just around the corner. Tet exposed that promise as hollow.

The turning point came when Walter Cronkite, the most trusted newsman in America, delivered a rare personal verdict. On national television, he declared the war a stalemate and that it was unwinnable in any conventional sense. President Lyndon B. Johnson, who once boasted he had the backing of "Middle America" because of Cronkite, now reportedly muttered, "If I've lost Cronkite, I've lost Middle America." Soon after, Johnson shocked the nation by announcing he would not seek reelection.

Even as the US military requested 200,000 more troops, the political will to escalate the conflict was crumbling. For many in Washington, the Tet Offensive marked the moment the war stopped being about victory and became a question of how to get out.

During the tumultuous US presidential election, Democratic front-runner and brother of the late John F. Kennedy, Robert F. Kennedy (RFK), fell to an assassin's bullet. A rather lackluster Democrat nominee was picked: Hubert Humphrey. The election was ultimately won by Republican firebrand Richard Nixon.

Nixon would later be cast as a political arch villain because of the Watergate scandal. However, if Nixon understood anything, he understood international politics. He knew that Vietnam was a mess, and he came into office seeking earnest solutions to end the conflict as quickly as possible. He spoke in terms of "peace with honor" and of the need to utilize a "Vietnamization" strategy.

President Nixon understood that US troops propping up an unpopular regime and a hated South Vietnamese military would never win over the people of South Vietnam. As such, he worked to get the Vietnamese people more involved with their own governance, their own defense, and, to put it bluntly, their own problems. He knew that America could not play watchdog and clean up the mess that South Vietnam had become. There had to be a slow, concerted effort to put more and more control into the hands of the South Vietnamese.

It is rather ironic that it came to this since that was all the people of South Vietnam (or any part of Vietnam) wanted in the first place. But due to centuries of French and then American interference, the government of South Vietnam had become such a corrupt mess that hardly anyone could trust it. Nevertheless, Nixon began the tough process of decoupling from Vietnam. Starting his first year in office, in 1969, he began to withdraw the buildup of US troops, which had ballooned into the hundreds of thousands under LBJ.

That summer, Nixon withdrew some 25,000 US troops from Vietnam, leaving an estimated 475,000 still in place. This was part of his new policy of "Vietnamization"—the idea that South Vietnamese troops would gradually take over the fighting. Yet, the war showed no signs of letting up. North Vietnamese and Viet Cong forces kept up the pressure with attacks and ambushes, while American forces tried to hold the line even as the gradual pullout began.[48]

That very year, the long-time leader of the North Vietnamese—Ho Chi Minh—passed. He was a relatively old man at this point, as he was seventy-nine years old, but it came as a shock all the same. Many openly wondered if perhaps his passing would somehow change the landscape of what was happening in Vietnam.

This was not to be, though. Even though he was certainly mourned by his supporters, one of his colleagues simply picked up the banner and continued right up where he left off. This is a clear testament to how strong an organization Ho Chi Minh had built since it was able to seamlessly continue even after he was gone.

---

[48] Karnow, Stanley. *Vietnam: A History*. Pg. 616.

In the meantime, Richard Nixon continued the pullout of soldiers. By 1971, there were only about 160,000 US troops left in Vietnam. Nixon, while drawing down troops, tried to heavily invest in the military, government, and infrastructure of South Vietnam, hoping to fortify it enough to stand on its own.

Many in South Vietnam began to see the writing on the wall. They realized that the Americans were leaving, and even those who tried to be loyal to the South Vietnamese government's cause were living in constant dread of what would happen if the US presence was completely removed. They knew that as soon as the US removed its forces entirely, there would be nothing to stop the North from coming down upon them in full force. For those who had long collaborated with the US, there was a natural fear that if the North toppled the government in South Vietnam, they would be put on trial as traitors. Considering all of this, a feeling of fear began to permeate into the hearts of many officials in South Vietnam, and attempts were made to delay the exit of US troops.

Paradoxically enough, even as Nixon was winding down the war in Vietnam, he briefly expanded it into the rest of former Indochina. He authorized secret bombing campaigns in both Cambodia and Laos, hoping to smash the cross-border supply lines known as the Ho Chi Minh Trail.

This move was widely criticized by the press at the time, with Nixon accused of going back on his promise to wind down the war and instead risking its expansion. Members of the media were not the only ones who questioned his judgment. Even within his own administration, voices of dissent emerged. His secretary of the interior, Walter (Wally) Hickel, issued a public rebuke of Nixon's handling of Vietnam and the unrest it was causing at home. Hickel soon lost his job for his trouble; he was dismissed before the year was out.

Hickel was not the only one with reservations. Petitions of protest circulated inside the State Department, with hundreds of staff registering their opposition to the widening of the war. Nixon, for his part, was ready to come out swinging. The day after the Cambodia campaign began, he set off his own firestorm of rhetoric at a Pentagon briefing, defending his decision to strike enemy sanctuaries across the border.[49] He was also ready to take on perceived enemies on the home front, as

---

[49] Karnow, Stanley. *Vietnam: A History.* Pg. 625.

was indicated in off-the-cuff remarks made in the hall in which he referred to anti-war protesters as nothing but a bunch of "bums" who were ruining what would have otherwise been good and decent college campuses of higher learning.[50]

All of Nixon's loose talk would come back to haunt him. On May 4th, 1970, angry anti-war demonstrators were fired upon by National Guard troops at Kent State University in Ohio, resulting in the deaths of four college students. Even though Nixon obviously had no control over such a spontaneous outburst of violence, people remembered his words, and his critics were eager to link him to what had happened.

Even worse, in the aftermath of the tragedy, his administration remained gruff and insensitive in its comments, inviting even more criticism. Soon, Nixon became the ultimate bogeyman of the anti-war movement. Perhaps no one voiced this more memorably than singer-songwriter Neil Young. His song "Ohio," recorded with Crosby, Stills, Nash & Young, left no question as to who was to blame, as Young wailed about "Tin soldiers and Nixon coming."

Yet, in a surprising twist, Neil Young's music would circle back to Nixon a few years later. In his 1976 ballad "Campaigner," Young added a line that stunned many of his listeners: "even Richard Nixon has got soul." It was not a pardon for Nixon's deeds, but it was an acknowledgment of his humanity. It was a remarkable departure from the fury of "Ohio."

Nixon was, of course, a deeply polarizing figure. He would have had detractors under any circumstance, but the divisive issue of Vietnam magnified everything, ensuring that for millions of Americans, he would forever remain the villain of the story.

The bombings did little to curtail the North Vietnamese. In the spring of 1972, the North Vietnamese decided to gamble big. Rather than sticking to shadowy guerrilla strikes, they rolled out tanks, heavy artillery, and well over a hundred thousand troops in what came to be known as the Easter Offensive. This was no hit-and-run campaign. It was an outright invasion, with columns of North Vietnamese troops pouring across the DMZ, others pushing through Laos into the Central Highlands, and still more surging up from Cambodian bases toward the Mekong Delta.

---

[50] Karnow, Stanley. *Vietnam: A History.* Pg. 625.

The South Vietnamese army, which Nixon had been trying to build up through his policy of Vietnamization, quickly found itself staggering under the weight of the assault. Quang Tri in the north fell, panic swept across towns and cities, and the ARVN seemed on the verge of collapse. For a moment, it looked like the whole façade of Vietnamization was about to come crashing down.

But Nixon was not about to let that happen. He answered with a massive aerial counterattack, unleashing Operation Linebacker. Day after day, American planes rained destruction on supply lines, bridges, and depots, even mining Haiphong Harbor and pounding targets deep in the North. South Vietnamese forces, bolstered by this wall of American firepower, slowly steadied themselves. At An Loc and Kon Tum, they dug in and held on, beating back wave after wave of North Vietnamese assaults.

By the fall, the offensive had lost steam. North Vietnamese troops were forced to pull back from much of what they had seized, though they still clung to some captured ground. The damage, however, was done. The Easter Offensive showed that Hanoi could launch a full-scale invasion, absorb some of the heaviest bombing of the war, and still fight on. The Americans had managed to stop them, but only with a staggering display of firepower. For the US, that was both a relief and a sobering reminder that the South could not stand on its own without US might.

The Nixon administration began to embark upon a carefully choreographed diplomatic course. Nixon had a diplomatic breakthrough with China, becoming the first American president to have an audience with the regime's communist leader, Mao Zedong. Nixon had it in his mind that if he could enter into a deal with Mao, he could use China as leverage to get a more favorable outcome to the Vietnam War.

Nixon just might have been on to something because his visit to China certainly got the attention of the North Vietnamese. The North Vietnamese could not help but take notice. At this stage, they were getting quite a bit of support from China.[51] Besides political and military support, the Chinese were crucial in supplying rice to North Vietnam. North Vietnam was not the rice bowl that South Vietnam was, so it had come to depend more on imported food. If Nixon had convinced the

---

[51] Karnow, Stanley. *Vietnam: A History*. Pg. 653.

Chinese to stop supplying rice to North Vietnam (as unethical as that might have been), that alone could have been a real game-changer.

Talks between the US and North Vietnam—pushed along by years of backchannel dealings between Henry Kissinger and Le Duc Tho—finally produced what was hailed as a breakthrough. On January 27th, 1973, in Paris, the Paris Peace Accords were signed. This agreement was supposed to mark the beginning of the end of America's combat role in Vietnam. Nixon wasted no time in touting it as his long-promised "peace with honor." The deal called for a ceasefire, the withdrawal of all US combat troops, and the return of American prisoners of war. On paper, it looked like a diplomatic victory for the Nixon administration. In practice, however, it left North Vietnamese troops firmly entrenched in the South.[52]

The American people clearly wanted out of Vietnam, and Nixon was attempting to provide an exit ramp. However, Nixon's triumph was quickly overshadowed at home. Even as the ink was drying on the Paris Peace Accords, the Watergate scandal began to consume his presidency. The irony was brutal. He had just won reelection in 1972 by a historic landslide, yet the break-in at the Democratic Party headquarters and the ensuing cover-up would destroy him. For a while, he tried to keep Vietnam on track, pointing to the agreement as proof of his "peace with honor." The deal did roll back American intervention and set a timetable for US troop withdrawals, but the fighting on the ground never truly stopped. Both Hanoi and Saigon broke the ceasefire almost as soon as it was announced.

By 1974, Watergate had exploded into a full-blown crisis. In August of that year, he resigned in disgrace. His successor, Gerald Ford, inherited the Vietnam quagmire and tried to carry forward what Nixon had started, but he did not have the authority or political capital to change the course of events.

Politically speaking, South Vietnam was a clear loser as it pertained to American politics. Both the Democrats and the Republicans were fully aware that the majority of the electorate wanted nothing more than to get out of the Vietnam War. Ford was well aware of this as he prepared for a 1976 presidential run, which would see him pitted against Jimmy Carter. As such, there was an increased eagerness to end the war before the

---

[52] Karnow, Stanley. *Vietnam: A History.* Pg. 669.

presidential election was underway. Ford had enough baggage due to Watergate and Nixon's freefall, so bringing the Vietnam War to an end would at least lighten that already considerable load.

Ultimately, the North Vietnamese closed in on South Vietnam in the spring of 1975. The end came fast. In late April, as Saigon fell, the world watched chaotic scenes of desperate South Vietnamese crowding into helicopters during the frantic evacuation of the US Embassy. The South's capital was no more. Once the North took over, Saigon was renamed Ho Chi Minh City. Ho Chi Minh had died in 1969, but his followers made sure he was honored in victory.

The 17th parallel was erased, the Vietnam War was over, and by July of 1976, the fully unified Socialist Republic of Vietnam was officially proclaimed.

Chapter 11: Reunification and the Path to Modernization

"I always thought I would become a scholar or a writer, but I've become a professional revolutionary. I travel through many countries, but I see nothing. I'm on strict orders, and my itinerary is carefully prescribed, and you cannot deviate from the route, can you?"

-Ho Chi Minh[53]

After decades of struggle, North and South Vietnam were united once again in 1976 under the banner of a communist state known as the Socialist Republic of Vietnam. Those unfortunate souls who had opposed the regime faced an uncertain fate. Many attempted to flee the country altogether. Droves of Vietnamese made daring escapes on watercraft, heading toward Hong Kong, Australia, the Philippines, and even the United States. These refugees became collectively known as the "boat people."

Initially, many communities welcomed the Vietnamese boat people with open arms. Many had sympathy for these fearful refugees and wanted to help them. As the years dragged on, though, and as wave after wave of refugees continued to arrive, sentiments began to change, and communities were not quite as welcoming.

---

[53] Karnow, Stanley. *Vietnam: A History.* Pg. 135.

The weariness of dealing with Vietnamese refugees seems to have been two-fold. First and foremost, there was the strain of dealing with an influx of people who had to be processed and mentored so they could assimilate into a new society. Such things are taxing on governmental systems and trying on people's nerves. Another aspect, most especially as it pertained to Americans' acceptance of Vietnamese refugees, was a deep sense of shame. America had lost the war, and seeing these poor souls fleeing from the enemy that American troops had failed to defeat was a stark and terrible reminder of that fact.

The North Vietnamese and the Viet Cong were the victors, and for a time, they were content to enjoy what they viewed as the spoils of their hard-fought war. However, the triumph of these conquerors was rather short-lived because just about as soon as Vietnam defeated the United States, its old nemesis, China, turned its wrath on the Vietnamese again.

Although it did not seem to make much headlines at the time (just about everyone was perhaps a bit tired of hearing about wars in Vietnam by this point), the Sino-Vietnamese War erupted in earnest in 1979. The spark that led to this conflagration came when Vietnam decided to invade neighboring Cambodia. They did so under the pretext that the Cambodian Khmer Rouge regime had been mistreating the Vietnamese minority living there. Cambodians had also been crossing the border and stirring up trouble by raiding local villages.

A map of the Sino-Vietnamese War.[31]

Even so, China did not approve of Vietnam's decision to strike Cambodia. It likely feared that the upstart Vietnamese would become troublemakers in the region. As the heavyweight communist nation, the Chinese decided to throw their weight around.

China also did not appreciate Vietnam's close bonds with the Soviet Union. It wanted to show Vietnam that the Chinese were the ones to whom they should look for guidance. Yes, as had been the case long ago, China was seeking to demonstrate that it was still the hegemonic power in the region.

This moment in history had an eerie familiarity to it; it was almost like a repeat performance with a new cast. Sure, China in the late 1970s was a communist regime rather than an imperial dynasty, but its actions in Southeast Asia seemed to echo centuries of precedent. For generations, China had loomed as the regional heavyweight among its smaller neighbors. Throughout history, various Southeast Asian kingdoms, including Vietnam, had operated within China's sphere of influence, often as tributary states. When one tributary overstepped or threatened regional stability, China had historically seen itself as the one to restore order.

So, when China intervened between Vietnam and Cambodia in 1979, it looked to some like a replay of that old pattern. Much as the United States styled itself as the "policeman" of the world, China had long seen itself—at least within East and Southeast Asia—as a regional guardian of balance. Whether that self-appointed role was morally defensible is another matter entirely.

Vietnam, for its part, claimed it was acting to protect ethnic Vietnamese and other civilians suffering under the brutal regime of the Khmer Rouge in Cambodia. That regime, led by Pol Pot, has since gone down as one of the most genocidal tyrannies in modern history. Yet this was the very regime that China stood behind.

To the Vietnamese, this was a bitter betrayal. Vietnam had received extensive Chinese support during its war with the United States, and afterward, it tried to maintain amicable relations. But as Vietnam's relationship with the Soviet Union deepened and as it took military action to oust the Khmer Rouge in Cambodia, China began to see Vietnam as a regional threat. Beijing feared that Hanoi's actions in Cambodia were not just humanitarian but part of a broader effort to expand Vietnamese influence in Indochina. Vietnam could possibly even absorb Cambodia into a pro-Soviet bloc. From China's perspective, this would disrupt the fragile balance of power in Southeast Asia.

In response, China launched what it called a "punitive expedition" against Vietnam in February 1979. The Chinese invasion shocked many Vietnamese, stirring old memories of earlier Chinese incursions into northern Vietnam. However, the Vietnamese response was fierce. What could have turned into a broader conflict soon narrowed into a brief, bloody war that lasted less than a month. While China inflicted heavy damage, it ultimately withdrew, leaving tens of thousands dead and stationing large forces near the border to send a message. Still, the fact that Vietnam stood its ground against the Chinese juggernaut became a point of national pride.

The aftermath left scars. Vietnam's economy, already strained by decades of war, was further battered. The government, following a strict model of centralized planning, implemented agricultural collectivization and fixed pricing policies. These efforts were modeled on other communist systems and quickly ran into trouble. With state-mandated prices set artificially low and surplus production confiscated, farmers lost their incentive to grow more than they needed. As a result, cultivation dropped, and food shortages became common. In 1980, official figures confirmed that agricultural output had fallen well short of government quotas.[54]

The year 1986 marked a real turning point, as Vietnamese officials finally realized that central planning was just not working. This led Vietnam to maintain the communist one-party state while opening itself up to a more capitalist, free-market-style economy. Vietnam was not the only one doing this about-face in the 1980s. China, too, was coming to realize the value of opening up its markets even while maintaining communist control of the government.

By the 1990s, Vietnam had moved toward a market economy. This has led to a real turnaround in the Vietnamese economy, with Vietnam becoming an economic powerhouse and one of the leading economies of Southeast Asia.

The other main problem Vietnam faced after unification was bringing together the two disparate cultures of North and South. For those in the South who remained staunchly opposed to communism—or were merely

---

[54] Goscha, Christopher. *Vietnam: A New History.* 2016. Pg. 591.

suspected of such—the future was grim. More than 300,000 people were rounded up and shipped off to "reeducation" camps. There, they were lectured in communist dogma, forced into manual labor, and often endured brutal conditions that left many broken in body and spirit.

Even worse were the so-called New Economic Zones that the regime established. Entire families were uprooted from their homes and sent into barren lands. Northerners were relocated southward, sometimes onto the very properties once owned by Southern families. Prosperity collapsed overnight.

But the challenges went deeper than economics. Vietnam had long been divided on cultural lines, and the effort to knit the two halves together was fraught with tension. In the early years, Hanoi dispatched its own administrators to run affairs in the South. They ruled with a heavy hand, and resentment quickly spread among Southerners who now felt conquered twice over—first by the North Vietnamese army and then by their new overseers.[55] Nevertheless, by the 1990s, Vietnam began to stabilize.

In 1994, US President Bill Clinton decided to lift an embargo that had been placed on Vietnam during the days of the Vietnam War. Clinton normalized relations between the two former enemies the following year. He even made the unprecedented step of visiting Vietnam in 2000. Since then, Vietnam has become an important trade partner of the US.

To the chagrin of China, Vietnam has emerged as a valuable manufacturing hub in recent decades. As wages and trade tensions made China less appealing, many companies began shifting production lines southward. Nike, the juggernaut of athletic footwear, now makes the bulk of its shoes in Vietnam rather than China. And Nike is hardly alone. Scores of other global brands have followed suit, seeing Vietnam as a cheaper, more stable alternative that helps insulate them from China's economic and political risks.

Demonstrating its clout as a rising economic power, Vietnam joined the World Trade Organization in 2007 as its 150th member. Its success has made it a rival with China and other neighboring powers, with which Vietnam has had a contentious relationship at times, to say the least.

---

[55] Murray, Geoffrey. *Culture Smart! Vietnam: The Essential Guide to Customs & Culture.* Pg. 36.

In more modern times, due to tariffs being leveled against China by the US administration, Vietnam has become an alternative to Chinese-manufactured goods. Vietnam is often seen as a loophole through which similar goods can be obtained without having to deal with the issue of tariffs.

In 2016, Vietnam's relationship was further normalized with the United States when the US began allowing the Vietnamese government to purchase military hardware. The notion that the United States would be supplying arms to communist Vietnam would have been absolutely shocking back in the 1970s. In modern times, though, Vietnam is viewed as a potential player and even mediator in the region. This was demonstrated in February 2019 when President Donald Trump attended a meeting in Hanoi with North Korean leader Kim Jong Un.

Nevertheless, Vietnam is indeed still a communist country with a one-party system. The Vietnamese people have a very limited set of civil rights. While some basic rights are given, there are severe restrictions on freedom of speech, freedom of the press, and the right to assemble to protest grievances. Religion is also greatly restricted, although the constitution vaguely asserts that, in principle, "freedom of worship" is tolerated. This is largely just lip service on the part of Vietnam's government since there are some rather serious restrictions on religion in Vietnam. For instance, major legislation passed in 2018 entitled "A Law on Beliefs and Religions" restricted these rights even further. All religious groups must officially register with the government, and if approved, they must be closely monitored in case they engage in anything deemed subversive or a threat to national security.[56]

Many supposed dissidents have been arrested in recent times for a wide variety of alleged crimes against the state. However, there is one bright spot for Vietnam under communism. As is typically true for most communist regimes, a general sense of equality was given to women. Prior to the advent of communism, women were typically beholden to their fathers, husbands, and sons. They had no real rights of their own. Communist doctrine insists that the genders should be equal. As of this writing, women have served in the highest levels of government in Vietnam, even holding the seat of vice president.

---

[56] Murray, Geoffrey. *Culture Smart! Vietnam: The Essential Guide to Customs & Culture.* Pg. 38.

Even so, some habits are still hard to break. For example, in Vietnamese culture, the middle name is traditionally used as a means of designating gender. Many women carry the middle name of "Thi," which is seen as feminine. Men also have their own subtle variations with their middle names, which can be seen as gender indicators. Younger generations of Vietnamese, who prefer to be gender neutral, typically drop these names altogether. Most prefer not to have such indicators on a resume, so they consciously choose to omit them.[57]

In more recent times, Vietnam has become a bit of a haven for private entrepreneurs. Even though the state is wary of philosophical and religious beliefs it deems dangerous, it is not against the capitalist desire to earn money from products, commodities, and services. Many entrepreneurs of all stripes have flourished in Vietnam.

Vietnam is currently an economic powerhouse. In 2019, its annual gross domestic product growth was as much as 7 percent. Vietnam is also a manufacturing hub and a global export juggernaut.[58]

Vietnam was hit by the pandemic starting in early 2020, and it remained a major challenge through 2021 and into 2022. That said, Vietnam managed to keep positive economic growth in 2020, even as most of the world contracted, thanks to strong containment. However, the economy and society still took a significant hit, especially in 2021 when outbreaks surged. By 2022, the country had begun to return to normalcy, and by 2024, Vietnam appeared to be on a more stable footing. If growth trends and economic reforms continue, it has the potential to be one of Southeast Asia's more robust economies in the coming years.

---

[57] Murray, Geoffrey. *Culture Smart! Vietnam: The Essential Guide to Customs & Culture.* Pg. 193.

[58] Murray, Geoffrey. *Culture Smart! Vietnam: The Essential Guide to Customs & Culture.* Pg. 42.

Conclusion:
What Does the Future Hold for Vietnam?

Vietnam is a country with a long history. It is also a country that has had a lot of problems. Many of these problems were foisted upon Vietnam from the outside, whether it was the Chinese intruding upon their lives, the Mongols, the Portuguese, the French, or an American-led intervention to manipulate Vietnam's system of governance. Vietnam has been through the mill, to say the least.

As such, nationalism and a strong sense of self-determination have become ingrained in Vietnamese society. Considering how successful Vietnam has become on the economic front, it could be argued that its people's sense of determination on the battlefields of the past has now been reborn in the marketplaces of the present. If Vietnam continues down this path, it could become one of the most powerful countries in the region. And if Vietnam plays its cards right, it's not out of the question that Vietnam might one day become one of the leading nations of the world.

One aspect of Vietnam that seems to be driving its success is its uniqueness. This uniqueness can be felt just by eating Vietnamese cuisine. Vietnamese food has French, Chinese, Indian, and even some American influences. Vietnamese food is as subtle as it is spicy, with a rich assortment of herbs, nuts, beans, and roots mixed in with every delicious dish. Many dishes are served with amazing French-style breads and pastries, which are all holdovers from the French colonial era. The way in which people enjoy this food is just as varied, ranging from tiny pop-up stalls in the middle of the street to extravagant five-star restaurants.[59]

Yes, Vietnam has been through more than its fair share of trauma, but there are good times in its history. And in case anyone is wondering, most Vietnamese do not hold a grudge or have an ax to grind as it pertains to their past conflicts. Despite the carnage of the past, there are no real hard feelings against the Chinese, French, Japanese, or Americans. Vietnam is actually known as one of the friendliest locales for tourists.

Of course, that's not to say Vietnam doesn't have its fair share of problems. The Communist Party still calls the shots, and stepping outside the boundaries they've laid down can come with consequences. This isn't the Cold War-era Vietnam of reeducation camps and hard labor, but that doesn't mean the government takes criticism lightly. Dissent is still tightly controlled, and those who speak out too forcefully, especially locals, may find themselves on the receiving end of a government warning, or worse.

For foreign tourists, run-ins with the authorities are rare, especially if you steer clear of politics. However, Vietnam isn't the place to go waving protest signs or trying to stage demonstrations; that sort of behavior will get you noticed fast. While a visitor is unlikely to be hauled off for "reeducation," they could still be pulled aside and given a stern talking-to or even deported if things get too heated.

So yes, the grip of the Communist Party is still strong. It is just exercised in a quieter, more polished way than it once was. Vietnam is still a work in progress. We will all have to wait and see where it leads.

---

[59] Murray, Geoffrey. *Culture Smart! Vietnam: The Essential Guide to Customs & Culture.* Pg. 107.

Here's another book by Enthralling History that you might like

Free limited time bonus

Stop for a moment. We have a free bonus set up for you. The problem is this: we forget 90% of everything that we read after 7 days. Crazy fact, right? Here's the solution: we've created a printable, 1-page pdf summary for this book that you're reading now. All you have to do to get your free pdf summary is to go to the following website:
https://livetolearn.lpages.co/enthrallinghistory/

Or, Scan the QR code!

Once you do, it will be intuitive. Enjoy, and thank you!

Further Reading and References

Florence, Mason. *Lonely Planet: Vietnam.* 1999.

Goscha, Christopher. *Vietnam: A New History.* 2016.

Karnow, Stanley. *Vietnam: A History.* 1997.

Murray, Geoffrey. *Culture Smart! Vietnam: The Essential Guide to Customs & Culture.* 2016.

Ngoc, Huu. *Vietnam: Tradition and Change.* 2016.

Stuart-Fox, Martin. *A Short History of China and Southeast Asia: Tribute, Trade, and Influence.* 2003.

Image Sources

1. https://commons.wikimedia.org/wiki/File:Tambour-song-da2.jpg
2. https://commons.wikimedia.org/wiki/File:T%C6%B0%E1%BB%A3ng_vua_An_D%C6%B0%C6%A1ng_V%C6%B0%C6%A1ng_t%E1%BA%A1i_%C4%91%E1%BB%81n_C%E1%BB%95_Loa,_%C4%90%C3%B4ng_Anh,_H%C3%A0_N%E1%BB%99i.jpg
3. Esiymbro, CC BY-SA 4.0 <https://creativecommons.org/licenses/by-sa/4.0>, via Wikimedia Commons, https://commons.wikimedia.org/wiki/File:Nanyue_map.png
4. https://commons.wikimedia.org/wiki/File:Hai_B%C3%A0_Tr%C6%B0ng_(tranh_%C4%90%C3%B4ng_H%E1%BB%93).jpeg
5. Ian Kiu, CC BY 3.0 <https://creativecommons.org/licenses/by/3.0>, via Wikimedia Commons, https://commons.wikimedia.org/wiki/File:Tang_Dynasty_700_CE.svg
6. Bùi Thế Tâm, CC BY-SA 3.0 <https://creativecommons.org/licenses/by-sa/3.0>, via Wikimedia Commons, https://commons.wikimedia.org/wiki/File:ChuaMotCot2.JPG
7. The original uploader was Chuoibk at English Wikipedia., CC BY-SA 3.0 <http://creativecommons.org/licenses/by-sa/3.0/>, via Wikimedia Commons, https://commons.wikimedia.org/wiki/File:Hanoi_Temple_of_Literature_(cropped).jpg
8. Javierfv1212, CC0, via Wikimedia Commons, https://commons.wikimedia.org/wiki/File:Map-of-southeast-asia_1000_-_1100_CE.png
9. Hữu Nhật, CC0, via Wikimedia Commons, https://commons.wikimedia.org/wiki/File:B%E1%BA%A3n_%C4%91%E1%BB%93_Vi%E1%BB%87t_Nam_d%C6%B0%E1%BB%9Bi_th%E1%BB%9Di_vua_L%C3

3%AA_Th%C3%A1nh_T%C3%B4ng,_v%C6%B0%C6%A1ng_tri%E1%BB%81u_L%C3%AA_S%C6%A1_n%C4%83m_1480.png

10 TRMC, CC BY-SA 4.0 <https://creativecommons.org/licenses/by-sa/4.0>, via Wikimedia Commons, https://commons.wikimedia.org/wiki/File:Map_of_Southern_and_Northern_Dynasties_of_Vietnam.png

11 Bjoertvedt, CC BY-SA 4.0 <https://creativecommons.org/licenses/by-sa/4.0>, via Wikimedia Commons, https://commons.wikimedia.org/wiki/File:Vietnam_19th_C_-_cross_in_rosewood_mother-of-pearl_IMG_9582_Museum_of_Asian_Civilisation.jpg

12 https://commons.wikimedia.org/wiki/File:Emperor_Gia_Long.jpg

13 https://commons.wikimedia.org/wiki/File:Minh_Mang.gif

14 Jesuits, CC BY 3.0 <https://creativecommons.org/licenses/by/3.0>, via Wikimedia Commons, https://commons.wikimedia.org/wiki/File:Tonking_martyrs-sepia.jpg

15 https://commons.wikimedia.org/wiki/File:Prise_de_Saigon_18_Fevrier_1859_Antoine_Morel-Fatio.jpg

16 https://commons.wikimedia.org/wiki/File:Hocquard_and_Tonkinese.jpg

17 https://commons.wikimedia.org/wiki/File:Nguyen_A%C3%AFn_Nu%C3%A4%27C_(Ho-Chi-Minh),_d%C3%A9l%C3%A9gu%C3%A9_indochinois,_Congr%C3%A8s_communiste_de_Marseille,_1921,_Meurisse,_BNF_Gallica.jpg

18 https://commons.wikimedia.org/wiki/File:Ho_Chi_Minh_-_1946_Portrait_(cropped).jpg

19 https://commons.wikimedia.org/wiki/File:Vietnam1954.jpg

20 https://commons.wikimedia.org/wiki/File:A-6A_Intruders_of_VA-196_dropping_Mk_82_bombs_over_Vietnam_on_20_December_1968_(NNAM.1996.253.7047.013).jpg

21 Axuanwei, CC BY-SA 3.0 <https://creativecommons.org/licenses/by-sa/3.0>, via Wikimedia Commons, https://commons.wikimedia.org/wiki/File:Sino_Vietnamese_War_1979_map_english.svg

www.ingramcontent.com/pod-product-compliance
Lightning Source LLC
Chambersburg PA
CBHW050335010526

44119CB00004B/153